THE MOTHERS OF THE NATION

& Other Essays

OTHER BOOKS BY DIANE ROTHENBERG

Friends Like These: An Ethnohistorical Analysis of the Interaction Between Allegany Senecas and Quakers (1976)

Symposium of the Whole: A Range of Discourse Toward an Ethnopoetics, *with Jerome Rothenberg* (1983)

THE MOTHERS OF THE NATION

& Other Essays

Diane Rothenberg

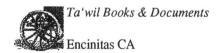 *Ta'wil Books & Documents*
Encinitas CA

ISBN 1-880280-06-X

CONTENTS

THE ECONOMIC MEMORIES OF HARRY WATT

SETTING

We first met Harry Watt in December, 1967. Stanley Diamond prepared a letter for us to carry along and telephoned ahead to introduce us. Diamond was interested in the experiments in translation that my husband, Jerome Rothenberg, was doing and thought that a meeting with some of the singers of the Allegany Senecas, a group among whom Diamond had worked, might be conducive to further explorations in translation. Harry Watt received us in his warm house on a very snowy evening and, because of his fond memories of Diamond, made an effort to acquaint us with the community. We went back several weeks later and the next summer rented a barely converted gas station just outside of the Steamburg relocation area. During that summer, Jerry engaged in productive translation projects with several of the leading singers and song makers, and our relationships with many people intensified and expanded. Toward the end of the summer, we were honored by clan adoptions in the Longhouse, and Harry Watt became my uncle in the Blue Heron clan.

We returned regularly to western New York in the following years to visit, to participate in ceremonies and to talk with friends. Some of the best talk was with Harry Watt. We would meet at his house, or around his sister's table, or, in better weather, at the old house, several hundred yards away through the woods, where Harry Watt and his wife had their gardens and where he most liked to be. This was the house that he had preserved when the forced relocation in 1965 caused by the building of the Kinzua Dam required that everyone occupying a house within the flood plain move. The misery of the time of removal was vividly felt, and the new houses generally resented. Harry Watt's old house was the almost singular representative of what had been a very recently transformed way of life and, as such, conveyed layers of meaning and emotion that we could hardly begin to appreciate. It was located high on a bank

This essay was originally written for the Festschrift, *Dialectical Anthropology: Essays in Honor of Stanley Diamond*, published by Florida State University Press.

overlooking the Allegheny River, with the gardens on one side and the woods all around, and Harry Watt would point to places when he talked about his childhood, about herbal knowledge, about encounters with animals. He talked about his experiences at the local Indian school and his running away from it for a perceived injustice, about his experiences travelling around the country doing construction work, about the skills and men involved in his work, about his encounters with Indians in other parts of the country, about Indian sovereignty, and about his hopes and fears concerning a retention of Indian identity by those who were losing the Seneca language and ceremonial knowledge. He talked about schemes for teaching the old ways, about his respect for those who were educated and knowledgeable in those ways, about his own sense of deprivation in having chosen paths which led him away from early immersion in Seneca language and culture, only to return in his later years with an eagerness and a sense of responsibility toward a goal of Seneca cultural preservation. Harry Watt's dedication in these matters was essential to the smooth running of the Longhouse Religion and, most importantly, to the preparation for the annual cycle of Six Nations meetings which preserved and carried the message of the prophet Handsome Lake throughout the intertribal circuit of believers. He was a model of a traditional Iroquois peace chief (although he did not have such a title): dignified, courteous, reasonable, personally available and generous, highly intelligent, and responsible to the collective. For these, and many other reasons, strangers were sent to see Harry Watt, and he was accustomed to representing his community to visitors—journalists, scholars, students. We witnessed many of these encounters and grew familiar with some of the regular turns the interviews would take, so that, over the years, we heard him discourse many times on some of the same subjects. Two of his favorites were religious epistemology and working, and I began to feel that I could "hum along" when he introduced one of these topics, although I tried not to seem inattentive and not to interrupt.

In June, 1972, we rented a house in Salamanca — on the Allegany Seneca reservation — for the beginning of a new project, this time the field work toward my dissertation. Again Stanley Diamond was most helpful, furnishing me with copies of his field data collected while he was attempting to assist the Seneca in their efforts to prevent the construction of the Kinzua Dam. The interviews and details of the community before the transformations produced by the relocation were useful to compare with my post relocation observations. We had no clear idea of how long we would stay, but the work was going well and there was no other place we needed or wanted more to be, so we stayed for two years. My own work turned more and more toward historical research and archives and away from a systematic accumulation and recording of field work notes. I regret now the tapering off of these detailed notes; when I reread them I hardly recognize my own voice, as if I were reading the experiences of some other person. Our social interactions and participation were intense, but became less instrumental, and the "participant" activity quite assuaged my early 1970's discomfort with the "observation" part of the anthropological enterprise.

Harry Watt frequently remarked that "people say I should write a book." I had heard that statement often enough to feel some impatience whenever I heard it again, but also to feel that maybe he really should tell the story of his life in writing and that I should help facilitate that ambition. While it also seemed to me that hearing a systematic account of life on the reservation at the turn of the twentieth century might be of use to my research, I was already more focused on the turn of the nineteenth century, so that my own goals were of secondary concern in this project. I offered to come around with the tape recorder that I rarely used, transcribe his recollections, and collaborate with him on editing them for potential publication. It seemed like a tidy project.

On November 16, 1972, I sat on the sofa in Harry Watt's living room, hunkered down for some serious descriptions of his early life on the reservation. He sat in his rocker, eyes slightly closed in an attitude of remembering and, to my distress, began, "When I was a boy, we really knew how to work." I had heard that many times before and I was sure that that was not the way to start this project. I tried to divert him, to suggest he talk about his grandparents, his memories of being a little child, events and people in his family. He responded briefly to my inquiries, but seemed determined to continue talking, in what seemed to me platitudinous ways, about working. The tape recorder ran on and he talked on, while I sat enveloped in a cloud of frustration. When he tired of talking, I turned the machine off, went home and transcribed what was on the tape, gave him a carbon of the transcription the next day, and never mentioned the autobiography again. My copy was filed away, and that other filing system in my head contained only a record of my frustration, amended slightly by my feeling of superior wisdom about what a real autobiography should be.

About five years later, friends who were editing an issue of a conceptual-art magazine, proposed that contributors from various disciplines should consider the subject of memory from the perspective of their own work. My experience with Harry

Watt's autobiography still rankled, and so I began an essay exploring the generalizing tendency of the elderly in relation to their own pasts and the related problem of using oral history as data. After I had completed several paragraphs, I remembered that I had the transcript in my files and thought to search it out for relevant examples.

Harry Watt's words flew out at me as a reproach both for my incomprehension and for the opportunity I had missed. The organizing principle of "work" was for him a primary value and a life metaphor. It was through working that he defined himself, and it was through the core of economic behavior that the rest of life was elaborated. Because I did not open my ears and my mind, as the Seneca invocation directs one to do, I missed the opportunity to know more about it. The transcript which exists represents in small measure an homage to the man who died in 1986. I include it as I have it to convey both the spoken cadences of the oral delivery and the richness of ethnographic detail.

THE TEXT

When I got a little bigger I worked, I had things to do. I always had things to do. When I got back from school I always had something to do. I started before I even went to school. I used to bring wood in. I had a bunch of sticks and carried them in. I piled them higher on my arms when I got bigger.

I carried wood and I carried water, helping my mother by bringing water. I carried water for her for washing and cooking. My dad used to tell me, "Always watch the water pail. If you see it empty, fill it up." He said, "Always have it full."

I always worked. For instance, milking cows; we had cows. I went after cows. And in the summer time, I had to go after cows. In the winter they didn't go out.

But as I grew older, there was more work. Many times when other kids would come along and ask me to go along with them, go fishing or go somewhere, "I can't go, I'm too busy." There was times when the kids would help me do something to get it done so I could go with them. Those kids didn't have the farm like we had. They didn't have no stock, and they didn't have to have chores. They had to get wood; we all had to do that. We all knew how to cut wood, how to use an axe. I knew how to use an axe by the time I went to school.

They all burned wood and they had to go out to cut wood. The wood near the houses was just brush and wouldn't last more than a few days. I went out to cut trees. Maybe they would be so big I had to cut them three times to get them into the wagon. I cut maybe seven, eight trees at that and that is a good wagon load.

I didn't have a saw. We didn't have power saws in those days. But there were hand saws that two men used together. But I went after wood alone with just an axe. I would hitch the horses to the wagon and used to go up the hill to cut wood. I would be wasting wood by cutting it and letting it lay there and rot, so we would cut it and then I would get the logs clear down to the foot of the hill, and then get the horses and load it up. It was work. I don't think anyone works like that now, today. One thing, though, I had to learn to harness the horses and there was a time I couldn't do it and when I wanted to use the horses, why the old man had to hitch them up.

In my family there was three more boys older than me. They went to school. I had one brother that went to Carlisle, the Indian school. And then another brother that went to Hampton; that's in Virginia. And the oldest one, he graduated that Quaker school. He graduated the eighth grade. A lot of them graduated from that school from the eighth grade.

But I, I didn't. I went to the Quaker school and then I got away from there. I ran away from there, after about three years. What happened to me some time ago I met a Quaker. He had my records, and he said, "Oh, it's you, Harry Watt. You ran away from school." I said, "Yes, I ran away from school; I didn't like the idea." I said, "I had to work all day and after that I was hungry and I was punished for something I didn't do and I was kept out until I was late. I was late and they didn't feed me. And I was hungry and I didn't like that. So I said to myself and four other boys, we got ready and we took off. And I never went back. I was sorry I didn't go back. Maybe I could have learned a little bit more. But instead I went to work." I came home and I told them what happened. Well, my dad wasn't too much about going to school and I suppose he thought if I went to work, why it would be that much less on his hands. So I went to work.

I was fifteen years old when I went to work. It was about this time of year, in the fall, when I ran away. And just about that time there was a man going around. He was looking for me to go to work. They were laying railroad tracks down to below our city. Petroleum Center is the name of the little town. They were laying railroad track there going down to Titusville. So I went over there looking for that man. I found that man and he said, "Yeah. How old are you?" "Oh, nineteen." Yeah, I lied four, five years. He looked at me. "Yup. You big enough. You be ready Monday morning when we start to go, your pay begins."

Oh, I was all for it. When we got there, you had to work. It wasn't too hard work, but I worked hard. My job was men's work and that is everything. I pick up rails and I had to learn how to drive spikes and I didn't know how to work with my hands with tools and I had to learn. But it didn't take too long. I knew how to chop with an axe, and use a hammer, and that helped me a lot.

We worked all winter and we lived in a camp. I often thought of that. Just the other day I said, "There's something I'm hungry for. We used to have at the camp, we had a man cook. He used to fry potatoes and bread crumbs and fish, canned fish. He would empty that fish in the great skillet where the potatoes were cut up and add some bread crumbs and cover it and let it fry. He had to turn it over. And the bread got kind of brown, toasted like and everything is brown and the fish get all mixed with the other things. Oh, I used to like that. I looked for that in the morning, for breakfast. You had to eat to work. In a place like that you don't get fat. You eat all you can; you wear it out. We come back for dinner. But when we had to go out, they had lunches in bags. They generally had a place, a shanty or two shanties, where we put our tools and they had a stove in there.

There was about thirty men from here. We had about three hundred men. I met a boy, he was a Mexican. There was a Mexican camp nearby. This boy, I see him quite a bit. There was a big store and we used to all go there. They had ice cream and all that and some of that candy. But this guy, he was about my age. He must have been, but I never asked him. He kind of liked me and he would try to talk to me and he couldn't because he couldn't talk English. There was a bridge close by there and we used to go to the bridge and just sit down there and let our feet hang down. And we'd talk. We tried to learn each other's language. I talked English and I taught him what to say, the meaning of different things, the names of things in the store. He asked me, "Cómo se llama?" I got so I could understand too. I could understand his language. I used to know quite a bit, but since that time I lost interest of it and I didn't see anybody I could talk to. But when I was talking to him, I could almost talk right along. He learned finally.

There were about one hundred Mexicans. And also Italians, pretty near a hundred of them too. And about a hundred Indians. Each group stayed apart and didn't mix. Oh, they had fights. There was two killings down there. The Mexicans had two or three and the Italians, they had some too. They killed each other inside the groups. In our group, there was two, killed in a fight. One of them was the cook. He was stabbed. The other guy, he was beat up and I think the train run over him.

I worked down there all winter and I got me some nice warm clothes, because I bought them myself. I always wanted some clothes, some warm clothes. I got my own money and when I got back I gave some to my mother. "Oh," she said, "I'll keep it for you."

After I came back from there I had cows and I had young stock and I had a horse. I kept the cows on my father's land; didn't have to pay him for it, but he used the milk. My first calf was given to me. My grandmother on my mother's side give me one when I was about eight years old. When I first went to school I had a horse, a little horse. I used to ride. The horse got bad after a while, but he lived quite a while. I consider myself a good rider. For a long time I didn't have a saddle, so I rode bareback. Finally I got an old saddle I bought myself. My father and mother, they saved their money and they worked hard. My father, he never went out to work for day's wages. He's working on the farm and what money he got, he went to work for others for a day or so at a time. But he had milk and from the milk he had an income. I remember when he had about thirty cows. We all milked. My mother used to milk, my sisters, my brother, myself. At first I had one cow I used to milk. That one cow, my sisters started in to milk that cow; my brothers started in to milk that cow. It was easy. After a while when you grab the teats, the hand gets strong from milking cows all the time. It's a lot of exercise. We used to have some hard milkers.

I had some cows. Oh, she was a good cow. I sold that cow and I got horses for it. I sold that cow and two yearlings and I got big horses out of that. They weighed thirty-two hundred pounds, about sixteen hundred pounds apiece. So they were pretty big horses. I worked them horses. I wanted them because if I had big horses I could do this and that. If I had big horses I could go and skin logs, go and haul lumber; I could go and haul wood. So the old man said, "You get yourself horses and a harness, and I'll buy the wagon." So one day I went shopping for horses. I bought this heavy pair of horses; made a trade. I got a good price on this cow because it was good. I told the man how much she give and he didn't quite believe it. So I said, "You come down in the evening and I'll show you." She used to milk two milk pails full of milk in one milking. I sold the cow to a guy named Underwood. He was a farmer and he was a dealer too. You have to watch how you dealed with them guys. I got a good deal. I told him that one of the heifers was coming in and it didn't come so he told me, "You got me." So I said, "It'll still come."

In those days I stayed home for a while after I came back

from working and I did a lot of things then. That was the year they started to pick up the track. There used to be a railroad track down to the park and when they got through with it and there was no more lumber, they tore up the tracks. And I worked there. And that was work. We used to pick up the rails and put it on the railroad car. After you got one up there, you give it a good push into the car. I used to get so tired, I slept at noon. There was an old man there I knew well, and wherever he said I should go I went there and I said, "Wake me up about quarter to one." And I'd go to sleep. I'd wake up, hurry up and eat, get through and get back to work. To get to work I had to walk several miles. I wasn't the only one who had to walk. Every day walk down there, work ten hours, walk back. When I get back, eat, sit around a little bit, then go to bed. That job lasted all summer and they shut down after it started to snow.

After that I worked on the railroad. I worked there for quite a few years. I can't describe exactly railroad work. Railroad work is a certain kind of work. When you work on the railroad, you don't do that on the farm. Railroad work is its own work. It's railroad work. We laid the rails, and then we spiked them. Gauged them, then spiked them. Sometimes we had to put down plates on the ties, and sometimes we put them every other tie. And there was times we had to put them on every tie; that's around a curve mostly. It's all heavy work. Sometimes we laid new tracks, sometimes maintenance. Sometimes maybe a broken rail. They get that rail out and put a new piece in there. Or else when just a piece off the end is broke off, then they cut it off and fit one in there. I've done that. I've stood on the railroad track and just pound, swing that pounder all day long. The first day you get awful tired, just don't want to get up the next morning. It hurts, hurts to move. My back hurt. But two, three days, maybe four days, you feel better. Finally it's gone. In the morning you wake up, and why, you feel just as good. You might feel a little tighter.

I worked uptown as a carpenter's helper and mason and I poured concrete and worked around concrete. And I did plastering. And that's hard work. That first day I thought my neck was broke. Sometimes when I get through with a job, by the next day I'd have another job. I'd heard about them by going around and different men would say, "There's a job over there." I'd keep that in mind and when I'd get a chance I'd run over there and, "Sure, come to work tomorrow." They were building houses quite a bit in Salamanca in 1917, 1918.

The old bridge went down in Quaker Bridge in 1917. That year we had a cold, cold winter. We had zero weather for about two weeks continually. One day it was about 35 below. I had a Model A Ford, a roadster, and the starter couldn't turn over. I had to crank, tup, tup, tup. It got started, warmed up and I went down the road. The people, some had cars, and they were cranking. The ice was four, five, six feet thick and when it came down the river it hit the bridge. It hit that bridge and the bridge lay on the ice and it carried it to an island down below, down to the point of that island and that's where it stopped. They got most of that iron. The bridge was built around 1878. The same company built the new one. The old one was wide enough for automobiles, but the iron that laid in there weren't bolted down and even the boards were not tied down. So when the cars came, the boards would loosen and slide one way and the other and finally they had to fasten them down. And the floorbeams began to slide off one way and the other and drop off. With the new bridge we put up, it was all concrete floor so it was solid. So that was my first bridge job. I worked with it until it got through. We finished it about the last of August 1920.

I worked the last day on that, and the next day I had a job over at the Quaker School. I painted the roof. They had a tin roof and they wanted that painted before it got too cold. I went and got a partner for myself and we painted the roof for about two weeks. There was a lot of roof there.

My father told me I should go into farming, but it's that payday. The railroad, they paid every two weeks, and the farmers they paid once a month. Only a few jobs paid once a week. There used to be a tannery in Salamanca and they paid every week.

In those days, after I came back from the railroad, I had horses. And I got a course from a school for horse trainers. I wrote for instructions and I studied and finally I graduated. I was a horseman. I could train horses, break horses to work. One time I had nine horses. I bought some, I traded some. In those days there were quite a few horse traders. I got into that a bit. I had two teams. My Dad used to use them but he had his own too. He always had his own.

Then I raised young stock. I raised bulls. One time I had four of them and they got to be a good size, about two years old. There was one of them that you just couldn't hold him in a fence. I was feeding them for meat and I sold them. I had to feed them at night and in the morning before I went to work.

In those days I used to watch the first automobiles come around, when I was eight years old. We used to see a truck come by. We used to hear that coming way down the road. Maybe two cylinders — chug chug, chug chug. And then we'd go down to the road and watch that thing go by. It had high wheels, same size front and back. And the motor was cross ways and it had a crank and a heavy chain in there. It made me think, standing there watching that car go by and I'd think, "Someday I'm going to have one of those. Someday I'm going to learn exactly how that thing runs." And I'd stand there and I'd think that, "Wouldn't it be nice if I could do that." Everybody'd say, "Harry Watt can fix that." I used to have that in mind. Finally I bought a car when I was about seventeen years old. When I was working on the bridge I got pretty good pay. On this bridge here I got about 60¢ an hour while the others were getting about 30¢, 35¢. Then when I worked for American Bridge Company I made $1.00 an hour. The railroads were paying around 30¢, that was good pay. I remember before I went to work, my brother was going to work on the highway, working for a contractor. It was good wages, $2.00 a day.

I was about the only one around here to go into iron work. Later on they did. Before the 1930's there were some from the other reservations who were iron workers. They were down there putting up a new bridge, just this side of where the Kinzua Dam is now, a railroad bridge. About four Indians worked there and that's about all the iron workers there were in them days. I would be the only Indian that worked on iron in some places.

THE COMMENTARY

Had I been listening, I would have realized that what Harry Watt was describing in his own life coincided with my interpretation of what the Seneca Indians had been doing a hundred years earlier — that is, adapting as well as they could to changes being imposed by the colonizers, while attempting to retain social cohesion, some measure of significant cultural content, and a sense of control. It is appropriate in the context of honoring Stanley Diamond for a lifetime of work that in large measure involved an examination of the consequences of capitalist colonial expansion, to discuss from this perspective a people that he knows well and on whose behalf he has worked.

My own investigation focused on a reexamination of the interaction of the Allegany Senecas and the Quaker missionaries who arrived in 1798 in response to the Seneca invitation to establish a mission. The Quakers came to "civilize" the Senecas and understood by civilization the eventual necessary goal of a commitment to "distinct property." From a matrilineal, communal society in which economic viability was achieved through a complementary division of labor, in which female horticulturalists produced subsistence crops while men engaged in cash derivative activities (we are, after all, talking about several hundred years of world market extensions into the American continent), the Quakers hoped to forge a society in which men would farm private property to be inherited by sons while women would engage in household tasks appropriate to the "gentle sex." (Rothenberg 1976, 1980.)

The Quaker goal of civilization through male agriculture and private property was not only an expression of an eighteenth-century agrarian idealism. It was specifically an imperialist governmental policy designed to open western lands for sale to settlers in order both to satisfy land hunger and to raise money to pay war debts. If Indians could be induced to farm, they would both be pacified and reconciled to drastic land reductions. But the federal government could not afford to fund the program, and so the Quakers undertook, as a private society, to accomplish these goals. I believe their willingness to do so was related to their need to restore their former position of influence, which had been diminished by their reluctance to participate in the American Revolution. (*Vide* Rothenberg 1976 for extended discussions of Quaker activities.)

Because the Quakers were an exclusive society proscribed from seeking converts, their emphasis was on assisting the Senecas in this world rather than in the next. Their emphasis, like Harry Watt's, was on appropriate work as a measure of human worth. They were critical of "idlers" and eager to reduce economic reciprocity and resource distribution. And they were very eager to move women into an exclusive domestic sphere. Harry Watt strongly objected to this orientation and used to say that he believed that a scrupulously clean house would indicate that a woman had wrong values. He recognized the important contribution of women to the life of the community in general and to the management and continuation of the Longhouse, and he predicted that it would be the energy and effort of the women upon which a continuation of traditional Seneca life would depend.

The centrality of the nuclear family reflected in Harry Watt's narrative was promoted by the Quakers and endorsed by the prophet Handsome Lake. The prophet's visions established the terms of social restructuring that are now the foundation of the contemporary Handsome Lake Longhouse Religion and of the conservative "old way" among the various groups adhering to that religion. Unlike the Quakers, Handsome Lake encouraged the establishment of clustered settlements, following the older residence pattern, and he rejected the Quakers' urging that economic reciprocity be abandoned, a goal to be accomplished through dispersed agricultural homesteads. Developments during the nineteenth century resulted in what William Fenton has called a "rural neighborhood" pattern (1967), with nodes of settlement occurring between dispersed homesteads. Osteological evidence from nineteenth-century cemeteries (Lane and Sublett 1972) indicates that these homesteads were patrivirilocal by contrast with the normative past of a matriuxorilocality, which was probably situationally variable over time.

The issue of whether males engaged primarily in agriculture as a result of the Quaker influence was a crucial point in my investigations. Harry Watt's father Hiram was, in fact, a farmer, although, as the narrative indicates, "What money he got, he went to work for others for a day or so at a time." According to his daughter, Hiram Watt was a first generation farmer who, as a destitute boy of twelve began to clear, and hence claim, available reservation land to support himself and his widowed mother. He did this after the 1860's, when dairy farming had become a viable industry for both whites and Indians. The coming of the railroads made possible the shipping of cheese produced in the local factories, which bought fluid milk. (Ellis 1879) As Harry Watt says, "But he had milk and from the milk he had an income."

The Quakers made much of the cultural inhibitions that men felt to farming, and the story of women mocking men who took up a hoe by themselves taking up a gun is an often repeated one. The evidence, however, reveals reasons more economic than cultural for men to resist farming. With an absence of access to markets for agricultural products, men could not generate the cash the community needed. Men engaged in whatever work they could find, which included farm work for wages — "it's that payday." Although dairy farming had become a cash viable activity, Hiram Watt's almost total dependence on farming was unusual among the Senecas. Harry remarks this when he contrasts his responsibilities with those of his friends who "didn't have the farm like we had."

Harry Watt's remarks about horses ("I wanted them because if I had big horses I could do this and that. If I had big horses I could go and skin logs, go and haul lumber; I could go and haul wood...") reflects a long tradition of the use of horses in the Seneca community. It was an ongoing source of friction with the Quakers. They encouraged livestock production but complained that cattle were neglected in the winter when men were away hunting. They also complained that horses proliferated in a way that was of no use to the community. Horses were of no use in such numbers if men were to concern themselves with agriculture, but they were of great use if the men were to engage in lumbering. Much to the Quakers' disapproval, this is what men did after 1812 and what the first white settlers did as well. The Seneca word for horse translates as "he hauls logs," and such crops as men raised, e. g. oats and hay, were associated with horses. The activities of the Indian and white loggers were intermeshed both in terms of labor and of access to the natural resource. Jurisdiction over the sale of logs from communal reservation land became a source of tension within the community, and conflicts over authority to alienate both land and natural resources were central to the displacement of the traditional political system of lifetime chiefs by the creation in 1848 of the Seneca Nation with its elected government.

Harry Watt's experiences as a laborer in western New York at the beginning of the twentieth century reflect the history of that region. Settlement of the area began late and slowly and relied on lumber. The convergence of three railroads, the Atlantic and Great Western, the Erie, and the Rochester and State Line, established the conditions for more rapid growth of the area around Salamanca after 1860. It was the route by which local products could be transported out of the area, and also the conduit through which oil from Pennsylvania was distributed (Ellis 1879). Employment was available not only in laying and maintaining track, but also in the repair shops, the car shops, and in the stockyards maintained by the railroads. Small factories with loading platforms facing the tracks were established. Although the area had been deforested by the late nineteenth century, bark stripping for local tanneries continued to provide work in the former forests. Wage labor employment was available in the expanding economy. Seneca women, using the skills they had learned at the Quaker School, were employed as domestics by local families. Indian workers provided a steady and reliable source of cheap labor. More highly skilled work paid better, but this was rarely available to local Indians. As a result, many young adults left the local area to seek employment elsewhere and frequently returned, if at all, only after retirement. Lack of suitable employment has been the cause of an ongoing drain of educated and able people away from the reservation community which needs them.

When Harry Watt remarked that he regretted that he hadn't gone back to school, he did not add what he so often did, that he also envied those who had never gone to school. In his later years, he came to believe that school learning was a

distraction from learning the intellectual content and practice of
the traditional Seneca culture and particularly of the religion. He
could speak Seneca, although not as well as he would have
wished, and he would note that speaking Seneca was a punish-
able offense at the Quaker school.

A formal school for children was established at Tunesassa,
the Quaker farm, in about 1816, and there were problems and
opposition to it from the beginning. The school became the
central symbol around which fundamental divisions in the
community expressed themselves. The situation became so
tense that by 1821 the schoolmaster felt his life threatened.
There were several abortive openings and closings and locational
shifts until the middle of the 1840's, when the Quakers con-
cluded that only a boarding school would reduce community and
home influences on students and permit the program of accul-
turation they were advancing. This school was a significant
experience in the lives of many now elderly Allegany Senecas,
remembered with both the pleasure and pain of most Indian
boarding school experiences.

Finally, Harry Watt's experiences with representatives of
the white world were ongoing and varied. So it has been from the
inception of the reservation in 1798. The reserved land is a strip
forty miles long and a half mile wide on each side of the Allegheny
River. Although they did not stay, emigrants passed through on
the river on their way west, and the Senecas used it as a highway
to bring trade goods to Pittsburgh and other centers. The shape
of the reservation made the Seneca country all boundary with no
interior, affording no place to avoid contact with whites and the
influences of white society. Harry Watt's early observations of
the automobile and the desires it provoked in him is an example
of that influence. The Quakers looked with favor on Allegany as
the site of a mission, because they believed it stood outside of the
area of white influence, and Handsome Lake had hoped to shape
his people into an encapsulated and protected community. Both
views were shortsighted; there would be no place to escape white
expansion. Colonization from the beginning necessitated continual readjustments. That the Senecas have remained a vital
social unit for so long is a testimony to their adaptability.

But Harry Watt was always concerned with the loss of
cultural content, a loss which he saw intensifying with technological development and language loss. The viability of the social
unit itself he felt to be tied to and protected by the intellectual
content of the culture. He used to say that at that time when
white men come around asking what it is to be a Seneca and no
one call tell them, then that will be the signal for the reservation

to be terminated. For Harry Watt, the final defense of Indian life depended on what people had in their heads and in their hearts.

REFERENCES

Ellis, Franklin. 1879. *History of Cattaraugus County, New York, with Illustrations and Biographical Sketches of Some of Its Prominent Men and Pioneers.* Philadelphia: L. H. Everts.

Fenton, William N. 1967 "From Longhouse to Ranch-type House: The Second Housing Revolution of the Seneca Nation." In *Iroquois Culture, History and Prehistory, Proceedings of the 1965 Conference on Iroquois Research.* E. Tooker, ed. Albany: New York State Museum and Science Service.

Lane, Rebecca A. and Sublett, Audrey J. 1972. "Osteology of Social Organization: Residence Patterns." *American Antiquity,* 37:2.

Rothenberg, Diane. 1976. *Friends Like These: An Ethnohistorical Analysis of the Interaction Between Allegany Senecas and Quakers, 1798-1823.* Ann Arbor, Mich.: University Microfilms.

_____. 1980. "Mothers of the Nation: Seneca Resistance to Quaker Intervention." In *Women and Colonization: Studies of Pre-Capitalist Societies.* New York: Bergin Publishers (Praeger).

THE MOTHERS OF THE NATION : SENECA RESISTANCE TO QUAKER INTERVENTION

The contemporary Allegany Senecas, whose reservation is located on the New York-Pennsylvania border in Cattaraugus County, are one of three remaining Seneca groups in New York State.[1] Together with the nearby Cattaraugus they made radical changes in their political organization and, in 1848, established the Seneca Nation; they have been governed by democratically elected officials since that time. The third group, the Tonawanda Senecas, declined to participate in the "revolution" towards electoral government and retained the older political system of appointed chiefs. Today, the combined population of the Seneca Nation is approximately 2,500 people; the Tonawanda number about 400. Economically the Senecas are integrated into the life of the surrounding semi-rural and economically depressed environment of western New York and are overwhelmingly wage laborers. They have retained some measure of social exclusivity, which is steadily diminishing as a result of modern technological pressures and integrated education. The site of the Allegany Reservation, which flanks the Allegany River for approximately forty miles, encouraged constant contact with settlers, who used the river for transportation. Superficially the Indian population is virtually indistinguishable from its white neighbors, but a considerable effort is being made to retain and transmit distinctive cultural features, including ceremonies and dances, language, and techniques of food preparation and crafts, all of which are seen to be endangered by the white "monoculture." One of the male leaders of the traditionalist Longhouse Religion remarked to me that, if the religion is to survive, it will be through the efforts of Seneca women.

THE SENECA NATION: PRE-NINETEENTH CENTURY CONTACT AND COLONIZATION

The Senecas constituted one of the Five Nations of the League of the Iroquois, which was expanded to include the Tuscaroras in

---

First published in Eleanor Leacock and Mona Etienne, eds., *Women and Colonization* (Praeger, 1980).

the late eighteenth century. Whether the League, a loose confederation of Mohawks, Oneidas, Onondagas, Cayugas and Senecas, was formed before Europoan influence was felt in the New World or in response to some of the new pressures created by the European intrusion is still conjectural. It appears from traditional accounts to have been created to reduce belligerency among the participating tribes, rather than as the offensive alliance it later became, and to have been in existence since at least 1450 A.D. Metaphorically, its structure was the longhouse, the matrilocal, multiple-family Iroquois residential structure which housed a matrilineally related group of women with their husbands and children. The Mohawks were guardians of the eastern "door"; the Senecas, located in the Genesee region, protected the western; and each tribe constituted one of the "fires," as each family unit did in the longhouse.

The principle guiding decision making in the League, as well as at the local level, was unanimity; majorities did not rule. The representatives of each group, sachems chosen by clan mothers, arrived at unanimous decisions in separate enclaves and then spoke as the single voice of their group. Whatever unanimity indicated, the machinery to enforce decisions was lacking. Only the coercive power of public opinion could control behavior, and the more distant the communities were from the central "fire" of the Onendagas, the more the influence of the League dissipated. Real action was determined and controlled by the local group. In the antagonism between the French and the English for hegemony in North America, the Mohawks in the east had strong ties to the English, whereas the western Senecas' trade connections allied them more often to the French. Enforcement of League decisions on those Senecas in the Allegany region and further west into the Ohio area — for all practical purposes quite out of reach of the western "door" from which they had exited — was especially difficult both because of the distances involved and because these Seneca colonies had interests frequently more coincidental with their western Indian neighbors than with their eastern confederates. Because of the strategic power of the League in relation to the colonial powers, concurrence of its members in most decisions was comnon, not only because it was expected, but because it was advantageous. When it was not advantageous, separate and contrary action would be taken in spite of the principle of unanimity.

Diane Rothenberg

The Effects of Trade and Warfare: Sedentary Women and Mobile Men

Both the strength of the League and the development of Seneca colonies west of their Genesee homeland are directly related to the economic activities and rivalries of Europeans and to the changes in natural resources which these activities effected. The thirty years following 1603 were a period of extensive Atlantic-seaboard settlement by Europeans who wanted furs, particularly beaver skins, for export. As George Hunt remarks, "Competition for trade was, or soon became, a struggle for survival" (1940:19) as Indians quickly became dependent on metal tools and firearms and lost skill in the manufacture and use of the older technology. It is apparent, too, that the group with metal weapons and firearms had a military advantage which had to be matched by any other group which hoped to survive.

Trade goods had an early and profound effect on Indian groups. European trade goods appear in Iroquois archaeological sites as early as 1570 in the Niagara Frontier area (White 1961). James A.Tuck, discussing archaeological remains dating before 1654, the date of the initial contact between Onondagas and Europeans, notes that

> steady decay in native arts and crafts provides a measure of the growing importance of European trade goods. Stone axes, knives and arrow points disappear and metal ones take their place. By the time of the first recorded contact between Onondagas and Europeans the native manufacture of pottery had become virtually a lost art. (1971:40)

By the 1670's European trade goods totally dominated the archaeological record and "virtually the only items of native manufacture found there are tobacco pipes" (:41). It is precisely this kind of involvement in the dynamics of trade that would influence the Senecas not only through the period of their expansion during the seventeenth and eighteenth centuries, but into the early reservation period as well.

Initially the requirements of the fur trade could be supplied from local resources, but the beaver was never abundant in New York, and by 1640 the local beaver supply was exhausted. The need to find new sources of supply led to a period of warfare and expansion — which removed men for longer periods of time and for further distances than had previously been the case, led to an intensification of the practice of adopting captives to substitute for men (or women) lost in battle, and probably resulted in an acquisition of more power and social control by women than had previously been the case (see Richards 1957).

Anthony F.C. Wallace provides a general description of the sedentary women and the mobile men of Iroquois society:

> It is not an exaggeration to say that the full time business of an Iroquois man was travel, in order to hunt, trade, fight and talk in council. But the women stayed at home. Thus, an Iroquois village might be regarded as a collection of strings, hundreds of years old, of successive generations of women, always domiciled in their longhouses near their cornfields in a clearing, while their sons and husbands travelled in the forest on supportive errands of hunting and trapping, of trade, of war, and of diplomacy. (1970:28)

This is a fair, normative description, but it shares the problem of all attempts to give an "ideal" cultural description in that it ignores the changes through time. Judith Brown (1970), who has properly related the powerful position of Iroquois women to their control of economic organization, consciously cholses to leave the time unspecified, although her data come from the seventeeth and eighteenth centuries. Richards, specifically concerned with the temporal problem, demonstrates the acquisition of more power and more local control by women during these two centuries (1957). What is obviously suggested is an increasing female control over local resources and local affairs as male activities associated with long-distance warfare and trade took men further away for longer periods of time. (See Ember and Ember 1971; Ember 1974).

The Mothers of the Nation: Women and the Land

Students of the Iroquois have evaluated the status of Iroquois women as high on various counts (Brown 1970; Carr 1883; Stites 1905), and the basis of their judgments directly or indirectly refers back to female control of the means, processes, and distribution of local subsistence production. The land "belonged" to the women: the concept of ownership, however, was not an Indian one and the issue became relevant only when sale of land to whites was a possibility (Brown 1970:159-60; Carr 1883:216-19;Washburn 1971; Wallace 1957; Snyderman 1961).

In council in 1791, Red Jacket, who was the sachem designated as the official speaker for the women, announced for them that "you ought to hear and listen to what we women shall speak... for we are the owners of the land and it is ours" (Snyderman 1961:20). This fundamental ownership was recognized by the revised constitution of the Seneca Nation of 1868. Although women were disenfranchised and the former, clan-based political structure, through which women exercised control by the appointing and removal of sachems, was abolished (Noon 1949:36), it was still required that three-fourths of the clan mothers consent to any decision to sell tribal land (Whipple 1889:399). In no instance does any authority suggest that land was legitimately under male control, but whites, of course, always assumed male control to be operative, and negotiations with Indian males for land sales was the rule.

In addition to the land itself, women owned the tools of agricultural production and food preparation, even when these tools were manufactured by men. Men's equipment was owned by men, but the distribution of the food products acquired with them (i.e., meat, fish, etc.) seems usually to have been at the discretion of the women. Certainly, women controlled the distribution of cooked food. Women also determined the distribution of surpluses, which would have come largely from their cornfields and which were stored in pits against times of shortages. This control has special significance, since it is likely that surpluses were exchanged intertribally (Parker 1912:34-36) and thus has implications for female participation and decisions in intertribal trade and politics. Furthermore, to the extent that war parties were dependent on provisions supplied by women, they could make significant determinations for or against military action by refusing provisions. Productive activities were carried on by work groups under the direction of a head women who was chosen for her ability by other women. This system provided frequent opportunity for female competence and experience to be exercised and rewarded by social recognition. The communal and cooperative work structure persisted long after the matrilocal residence pattern was abandoned. Writing in 1912, Arthur Parker described contemporary agricultural work groups under the direction of a head woman. Moreover, men who participated were under her direct supervision.

The presence of matrilocal, multifamily dwellings both facilitated such work groups and supported the independent position of women. These domiciles, which were built by the men but owned by the women and transmitted through the matrilineal clan, offered a maximum degree of protection to the women, whose husbands were frequently away, and provided the basis for the easy rejection of a husband who did not perform up to standards.[2]

While matrilocality provides a convenient residential arrangement to enhance female independence and to facilitate work groups composed of related women, any residential arrangement along with village endogamy (marrying within a village), would accomplish the same end. Men and women from the same clan were prohibited from marrying, but Seneca villages invariably contained two or more clans, and village endogamy was a frequent practice. William Allinson, a Quaker who visited the Allegany Seneca settlement in 1809, presents a description of the marriage and residential patterns of the time. His visit occurred eleven years after both the establishment of the reservation boundaries and the introduction of the Quaker missionaries, and by this time there appears to be a preferred pattern of virilocality (in which the wife goes to live at the residence of her husband) but within an apparently endogamous community. Allinson reports that marriages were arranged by the mothers or eldest sisters of young people on the basis of the young man's stated choice. A gift of trinkets worth approximately six to ten dollars was presented by the man and returned if his proposal was not accepted. If it was accepted, the mother of the girl then accompanied her to the house of the man, who was probably living with his mother, and left her there; but "as the Seasons for planting, hoeing, gathering corn, procuring Fire wood and other business came on, the female connections of the young woman assist her in the different operations during the first year at the end of which without any ceremony the marriage is considered valid & honorable" (Allinson 1809:55-56). These activities occupied much of the year and indicate the close presence of the girl's family. With endogamy as the general rule within a village with a clustered type of settlement, specific residence rules have little significance for work-group organization; related women could as well work together in one field even if they didn't share one roof.

Men's Activities and Economic Viability

While women were rooted to the locality and the annual agricultural cycle, men had a more flexible annual pattern in which to "hunt, trade, fight and talk in council" (Wallace 1970:28), but it is certainly a European bias that minimized Indian males' contributions to subsistence. The distortion is exemplified by Martha Randle's contention that "men's hunting added an important relish to the diet. A good meat provider was considered the best husband. But hunting was more a prestige and recreation point than a necessity" (1951:172). If this were true before the coming of Europeans, we cannot verify it, but it is a totally inaccurate evaluation of the importance of men's hunting during the period of European colonization. I would insist, on the contrary, that it is important to realize that the postconquest hunting activities of men contributed a crucial element to overall subsistence, not in terms of protein, which women and children could and did provide for themselves at least by fishing (Quain 1937:251), but in terms of trade goods and cash to purchase those trade goods which women's activities, on the whole, could not generate. Furthermore, the women recognized the essential contribution the men were making and encouraged them to continue it. The trivializing of this aspect of the economic organization reduces the insistence of women on maintaining their control over local agricultural production to a kind of senseless conservatism, if not virtual martydom, perpetuating a system in which women performed as slaves to self-indulgent men. It seems likely that the prejudiced statements made by white observers about a division of labor which was foreign, and hence pernicious, to them worked to devalue the importance of hunting as a real economic activity; these evaluations have been too easily accepted by social historians as a reflection of Indian reality. It is on these very judgments, in fact, that white rationales for restructuring Indian societies frequently were based.

Although domestic manufacture (particularly of artifacts made of wood and corn husks) did not disappear, and some of this technology has continued until the present, it would be difficult to exaggerate the Indian dependency on trade goods which was created by the fur trade, by European gift-giving diplomacy (see Jacobs 1950), and by a deliberate policy of generating colonial markets for the products of England's industrial revolution, particularly hardware and textiles. The Iroquois, in their strategic position of power balancing between the French and English until the defeat of the French in the 1760's, were the recipients of vast quantities and varieties of goods. These included not merely the finery, trinkets and liquor often cited and regarded by whites as easily expendable by the Indians when their access to these goods was reduced, but the firearms, ammunition, metal tools, and metal kettles that became essentials in the Indian communities from which the old technology rapidly disappeared. The ceremonial dress of contemporary Seneca women is not a skin garment from some long forgotten past, but a calico dress derived from the textiles brought in through the fur trade.

For the Senecas of the late 1790's and early 1800's, whose political importance had disappeared and who were no longer the recipients of gifts, cash or cash substitutes were their only access to essential trade goods, and it was men's activities which provided these resources. A Pittsburgh merchant describes what the Senecas brought for trade in 1803: "They generally came down twice a year, with their canoes heavy loaded, with furrs, peltry, mogasons, deer hams, tallow, bear skins" (Wrenshall 1816: 125-26). For the period around 1816 these products were supplemented by additional ones produced by men, and Wrenshall remarks that

> They have besides a sawmill, and being surrounded with lofty pine trees, they cut them into boards or scantling and float them down to Pittsburg at the time of high water. And on these rafts they bring their peltry, furrs, and good canoes, to push up their return cargoes ... and sometimes shingls, the latter of which I have bought for one dollar and fifty cents per thousand and paid for them in merchandize (:131).

These trade goods were the products of male activity, necessary to the economic viability of the community and made possible because women were engaged in subsistence and agriculture.

While the physical labor that women were observed to perform and their deference to men in such matters as eating order inclined some white observers to regard their position as subservient to men (e.g., Morgan 1851), refutations of this evaluation by other observers (see Heckewelder 1817) are numerous. The most famous assessment of the life of a Seneca woman was supplied by a female participant in that life of the pre-reservation period, who compares the burdens of Seneca women favorably with those of white women. Mary Jemison, the white captive, recalls:

> Our labor was not severe, and that of one year was exactly similar in almost every respect to that of others, without that endless variety, that is to be observed in the common labor of white people. Notwithstanding the Indian women have all the fuel and bread to procure, and the cooking to perform, their task is probably not harder than

that of white women who have those articles provided for them; and their cares certainly not half as numerous, nor as great. In the summer season we planted, tended and harvested our corn, and generally had our children with us, but we had no master to oversee or drive us, so that we could work as leisurely as we pleased (quoted in Seaver 1961: 55).

THE SENECAS AND THE QUAKERS

The life of the Indians entered a new period of adjustment with the defeat of their English allies in the Revolutionary War and with the introduction of new policies and new goals by the United States. Systematic losses through treaties and sales constricted their land base and, in 1798, the remaining land was being surveyed to establish reservation boundaries, In this same year a group of Philadelphia Quakers established a mission among the Allegany Senecas.

Seneca Strategy and Quaker Motivation

The Quakers came to the Seneca community by invitation. Indeed, throughout the 1790's the Allegany Seneca leader Cornplanter had sent repeated appeals for white assistance to the government of Pennsylvania, (e.g., McAllister: March 2, 1790), and the arrival of the Quakers was well received; the Senecas made every effort to encourage them to remain. The reason for Seneca receptivity that is commonly given is that the Indians were eager to receive instruction in white technology, but, in fact, only variable interest was shown in what the Quakers wanted to teach. It seems apparent that the Senecas envisioned the Quakers serving other important functions. The Quakers were a potential source of necessary services (such as blacksmithing) and of trade goods, not only through gifts but, it was hoped, through the establishment of a local trading post. The isolation of the Allegany Senecas was a mixed blessing, and the leaders of the community saw a great advantage in having local trading facilities which would reduce the need for men to travel to distant markets, where they frequently had trouble with white men and almost always procured liquor. Although some Quakers understood the benefits of establishing a local trading post[3] the proposal was rejected by the administrators of the mission (Indian Committee Collection Report: Box 2. Dec. 14, 1803).

They were willing to give necessary tools and equipment as gifts at first, and newly introduced activities (such as spinning) were initiated with Quaker-supplied materials as inducements; they were, however, reluctant to continue supplying material goods which they claimed produced a state of dependency among the Indians, and they refused to maintain a store. Their decision committed the Indians, necessarily, to distant markets and male mobility.

Even if the Quakers were not a source of supply, their presence was still essential to the Senecas. Indian lands were under continual pressure from white interests, and the Quakers — as the trusted, locally established, and respected representatives of the dominant society — offered the Senecas the most immediate protection from white chicanery. White settlement of the area was late in coming and not really underway until after 1816, but by 1809 the Ogden Land Company was actively engaged in attempts to acquire Seneca lands to which the company had bought the pre-emption rights.[4] Although the Senecas did not absolutely trust the motives of the Quakers and repeatedly asked for assurances that they would make no claims on Seneca lands as payment for services rendered, the Senecas had little choice but to encourage the continued presence of the Quakers to intercede for them on all levels of white society. The strategies adopted by the Senecas represent a response to a number of interconnected problems: protection of their lands, which required that they encourage the Quakers; the demands of economic viability, which frequently forced them to act contrary to Quaker advice and threatened to alienate the Quakers from them; and a changing environment, particularly with reference to white settlement and white markets, which required a flexibility on the part of the Indians in order to make rapid and appropriate adjustments.

The Quakers came to their missionary task with a clear and evolutionary notion of what constituted cultural and social progress and with a commitment to lead the Indians through those necessary steps — including a conversion to male agriculture from which would follow a love of private property — which they understood to be definitionally intrinsic to the state of "civilization." Fundamental to this goal was the restructuring of the village-oriented, matrilineal, extended kinship unit with a philosophy of economic reciprocity in favor of nuclear families living on isolated homesteads, conserving their resources within the nuclear family, and with men farming lands that their sons would inherit. Women were "to turn their attention to the business of the house, and the concerns more properly allotted to females in all civilized societies" (Jackson 1830:50).

Unlike other missionaries, the Quakers did not come to convert the Indians to Christianity; perhaps this is why we tend to assume that their judgments and observations were more reliable than those of other missionaries. Although they assumed that such a religious commitment would come with the accomplishment of civilization, the Quakers were by then an exclusive religious and social sect, with birthright and not conversion the basis of membership (Sydney 1963:327). Their efforts, as a result, were directed towards the socioeconomic life of the Indians and not toward their spiritual life. Any resistance to Quaker proposals for such restructuring was interpreted by them as the result of "habits of mind" (i.e. culture), laziness, or maliciousness on the part of Indians (or sinister whites). Although the Indians were prepared to entertain the possibility of alternative strategies in their attempt to achieve social and cultural survival, the Quakers understood no alternatives to their concepts of progress and civilization.

"A Nation of Farmers:" The Quaker program and the Seneca Response

The crux of the Quaker program was the removal of women from agricultural activities and the establishment of men in their place. To justify the continuation of the mission and to insure its continued support, it was necessary to see evidence that this goal was being achieved. Frequently students of the Senecas have uncritically accepted Quaker claims of success at face value, and Anthony F.C. Wallace tells us, for instance, "Now, and suddenly, they embraced the rural technology of the white man and became a nation of farmers" (1970:310). The same series of Quaker letters and reports which give indications of success, however, give many instances of discouragement and failure. What the Quakers took to be signs of initial sucess, such as male activity in land clearing, somehow did not result in the desired end. For instance, the visiting Quaker Committee in 1817 remonstrated the Indians, saying:

> You are very capable to calculate what is for your advantage and what is not. We therefore desire you would take into consideration whether you would not have been in a better situation generally if you had employed the same time which you have spent in cutting and rafting timber in cultivating your

good land....Yet it is evident their attention to cutting and rafting pine timber has much retarded their progress in agriculture. (I.C.C.: Box 3. October 16, 1817)

If the Quakers converted the Senecas into a nation of male farmers, it was a most temporary conversion. Evidence indicates that although subsistence farming (by women) continued, and some few men became successful farmers, the vast majority did not farm as a primary economic activity. In 1893 the Indian agent wrote that "the people on this reservation are not as a rule engaged extensively in agriculture....[They] have recently begun to develop their lands, having for many years supplied their actual necessities by selling timber, bark and ties. They have been making fair progress in farming for two or three years past" (Adams 1893:38). Whatever future prospects may have seemed likely in 1893, Dorothy Skinner wrote in 1929, "the Indians of the Allegheny Reservation do very little farming at the present time. They do laboring work at the various small towns near the reservation" (1929:1). And, if we did not know that the following testimony was dated August 23, 1920, we might suppose it was at least 100 years earlier, for Mr. John Van Arnum appealed to the Everett Commission, which was investigating the condition of the New York Indians, in the following terms: "We can hunt nor fish no longer, give us education to help us live. We need knowledge in agriculture work to develop our lands....It is education we need in agriculture so that when the young arise to become citizens, we can compete with any man." (Quoted in Everett 1922:191).

When Cornplanter appealed for white aid in the 1790's, he did so in the same terms as Mr. Van Arnum, referring to the disappearance of the game; but year after year the Quakers reported the men away hunting in the winter time, which invariably interferred with what the Quakers wanted them to be doing. In 1805, Seneca men were unavailable for employment by the Quakers, who had to find non-Indians to assist them; in 1807, cattle died because of lack of attention while the men hunted. The ability of Seneca males to prosper by hunting through this period is attested to by the report of John Norton, who visited the settlement in 1809. Because his assertions are so different from those usually advanced in support of Quaker claims, I will quote them at length:

These people have an advantageous situation; although their Reserve is only half a mile on each side of the river, for forty miles in length, yet it takes in the most valuable kind of land, and that purchased by the people of the United States adjoining to it, being rough and broken, and not likely soon to receive inhabitants, forms the most valuable hunting ground of any possessed by the Five Nations. They can conveniently take skins, meat and timber, to Pittsburgh, where they generally get a good price for these articles; the distance is only about 150 miles, and when the water is high, they can descend with Canoes or boats in two or three days....Our Host told me that Friends had taught several of their people to plow, and to do Blacksmith work, and some of their women to spin....but that many found it more to their interest to hunt than to work; that for his part he had acquired all his property by hunting, and that with the produce of the Chase, he had hired people to build and work for him (1970:9).

Norton noted that his host was the wealthiest man in the community. It was not the disappearance of local fur resources but rather the embargo of 1808 — when the United States closed North American ports to English ships and, by so doing, eliminated markets for furs — that forced Seneca men to find new cash-producing activities. Markets for agricultural products were not locally available and the means for transporting these to distant markets did not exist; agriculture would not answer. Not surprisingly, the new resource that was exploited was lumber, which stimulated the initial white settlement of the area. At first the Indians cut and rafted lumber for themselves; by the 1830's they constituted a labor force for white entrepreneurs and gained a reputation as excellent raftsmen (Kussart 1938). These cutting and rafting activities were more intensely deplored by the Quakers than the reliance on hunting had been. It represented a new way of continuing the pattern of sedentary, agricultural women and mobile, cash-producing men, which the Quakers had hoped would become obsolete with the hypothetical vanishing of game.

Because I am proposing an explanation of Seneca behavior which favors regarding them as rational actors, it is appropriate to consider briefly an alternative explanation of this same behavior which has been much favored. The Quakers called it their "habits of mind," and anthropologists call it "cultural persistence." But whatever it is called, the argument is advanced that resistance to Quaker teachings and advice stemmed from the hold that previous behavioral patterns exercised on the Seneca population, a resistance to change and a selective preference for new activities which would conform in structure to traditional activities. Morris Freilich (1958:473-83) has argued that contemporary Mohawk males engage in high-rise steel construction work because such an activity, with its excitements, dangers, and geographical mobility, structurally resembles the older warrior patterns through which men acquired prestige — that in effect, the older activity is replaced by a structually comparable new one because it offers similar psycholgical compensations.

Although it would be foolish to suggest that culture does not influence behavior, the Seneca evidence demonstrates time and time again flexibility and receptivity to new ideas, techniques and behaviors which would belie the assertion that the Senecas were bound within the tight constraints of a previous culture. It was almost axiomatic among whites that Indians would not work for wages, but in 1810 many young men became wage laborers and wage labor activity became the primary source of employment in the nineteenth century, not in the spectacular short-term contract employment of high steel work but in the steady employment offered by the railroad and growing local industries. Although women mocked men who took up the hoe, they themselves took with enthusiasm to the new skills, which involved novel motor habits, such as spinning, knitting and weaving taught by the Quakers. Insofar as culture conditioned their cognitive context, the Senecas must have preferred activities which were familiar in that context, but the culture model's inability to account for change and for novel choices forces us to reject it as sufficient explanation and to consider the influence of culture as one of many variables that explain behavior.

The Quakers, as we have said, were initially received by the Senecas "with an apparently hearty welcome, and treated with kindness" (I.C.C.: Box 1. May 11, 1798). Acting as spokesman for the group, Cornplanter extended total freedom of land utilization to the Quakers. When the latter indicated that they had sent a boatload of goods which had not yet arrived, they were loaned Indian tools and presented by the women with the seeds of "corn, potatoes, beans, squashes, and a variety of other garden seeds which they presented as a present to Friends, observing 'that it was very hard to come so far and have nothing to begin with'" (Jackson 1830:32). The Quakers purchased a small house from the woman who owned it along with her daughter.

A reciprocal exchange was maintainted throughout the summer. Halliday Jackson noted that "a great number of them came flocking about Friends, especially the women, who appeared kind and respectful, frequently supplying them with venison, fish, strawberries, and such other delicacies, as their country afforded" (ibid.). We should note that the inclusion of venison suggests the control that women had over the meat procured by the men, as well as over their own products. In exchange, the Quakers distributed "useful articles, such as needles, thread, scissors, combs, spectacles, etc., which were sent for that purpose, and were received by the natives with lively marks of gratitude" (:32-33).

Although the women were very eager to observe the Quakers' agricultural practices, they wanted this information for their own use. As Wallace tells us, "agriculture by men had been resisted as an effeminate occupation with the women themselves taking the lead in ridiculing male farmers as transvestites" (Wallace 1970:310). Allinson illustrates: "If a Man took hold of a Hoe to use it the Women would get down his gun by way of derision & would laugh & say such a warrior is a timid woman" (Allinson 1809:42). It is women who mock men; men seemed not to have any stake in other men's experimenting with farming. The women seemed to have no objection to men learning to plow fields that the women would then work, and men had always assisted women in the preparation of fields by clearing land and burning the timber and brush (Parker 1912:21). In the spring of 1801 an experiment was conducted whereby every other row in a cornfield was prepared with the plow; the alternating rows were prepared in the traditional manner. The advantages of the plowed rows in terms of increased yields were apparent, and thereafter the plow was increasingly used for field preparation.

In general, aspects of the novel agricultural activities that were introduced were selectively adopted by the men. In spite of the fact that there is no physical reason why women cannot plow, Quaker instruction in its use was exclusively directed toward Seneca men. But plows and oxen to pull them were scarce and expensive commodities. By 1811 there were only six yoke of oxen and four plows, owned as collective property (I.C.C.: Box 2. February 12, 1811), and wages were earned by those men who were able to plow for others. In 1819, for instance, it was reported that a young man had plowed twenty-two acres for other Indians at the rate of two dollars per acre (Society of Friends 1840:138), and plowing thus became, not an early step in a total male agricultural cycle, but a specific cash-producing activity.

Animal husbandry was another activity in which men were actively engaged, which initially the Quakers applauded as leading to their social conversion goals, but later deplored as being diverting. By 1817 the Quakers were saying that "they have more horses than is of any advantage to them" (I.C.C.: Box 3. October 16, 1817), although it seems likely that the Indians needed the horses for hauling lumber, a pursuit the Quakers found objectionable. Animals were raised for sale — "they have a number of fat cattle to sell this fall and hogs in abundance" (I.C.C.: Box 2. November 2, 1805) — and in 1814, when Halliday Jackson noted that little agricultural progress was being made, he observed that there had been a rapid increase in the number of swine which were not only salted for family consumption, but also raised and sold for the rapid income they would produce.

A distinct association of crops with one or the other sex developed among the Senecas; corn, beans, squash, potatoes, and vegetables in general, were raised by women, and animal fodder crops, particularly oats, and some wheat and hay were raised by the men. This is the same general pattern described by Shimony with reference to the Six Nations Reserve in Canada (1961:154-55). That corn remained a woman's crop is indirectly confirmed by a typical statement made in 1810 which reports that "several of their men have sowed spring wheat this season, and we believe an increasing disposition prevails amongst them to render assistance to their women in the planting of corn" (I.C.C.: Box 2. June 16, 1810). Corn remained the main food crop and was the crop most often mentioned as being sold to whites.

The Selective Conservatism of Seneca Women

While women conservatively retained their former agricultural control, they eagerly made themselves available to the Quakers to be taught a whole new range of additional skills — soap making, knitting, household management skills, and others — and they added the new tasks to the old ones. That the Quakers, in their professed desire to relieve women of onerous tasks, probably merely added a whole new set to the old ones is an interesting possibility. (Recall Mary Jemison's description of the life of a Seneca woman as pleasant, productive, and not excessively burdened when compared with that of white women of the same period.) Under the Quakers' direction those household chores that had been casual were encouraged to become a focus of compulsive attention, but we may assume that the continuing criticisms of an overall "negligent" attitude toward housekeeping reflected the firm grip that Seneca women kept on the reality of important versus trivial activity.

When spinning and weaving were introduced in 1805 the women were receptive, but the activity was relegated to the leisure-filled winter season. The new activities were organized along the lines of traditional women's work groups, and in this context the women responded positively to the new activity. The public support by head women under whom the others worked proved invaluable to the Quakers when opposition arose to the teaching of spinning; because of this intervention, the activity was continued. Only one woman became a proficient weaver, and she quickly turned this skill to a cash advantage by selling her products to white neighbors. Her elderly husband assisted her in this activity, but in a minor role (I.C.C.: Box 2. September 20, 1811). By 1820 the interest in spinning and weaving had disappeared (I.C.C.: Box 2. April 15, 1820), because, I believe, not only of the relocation of the activity to the private and unsocial domestic environment of the home (once there were enough spinning wheels to go around) and away from the social environment from which women derived much pleasure and prestige while working, but even more as a result of the Quaker refusal to continue to supply the raw materials, the acute problem of the procurement of raw materials in other ways, and the easy availability of more attractive commercially produced textiles which cash could purchase (Hedrick 1933:164).

The second area of female "conservativism" in relation to Quaker social restructuring emerged over the issue of private property. The division of the reserved land held communally by the Senecas into privately owned property was a fundamental goal of the Quaker program from its inception, but initially the Quakers demonstrated a sensible, gradualistic approach, believing that a commitment to private property would develop out of economic restructuring. But the failure to induce men to farm, apparent by 1816, persuaded the Quakers that a concerted campaign to divide the land into private lots and transfer control to the men was absolutely necessary. This action, taken at that time, was triggered by the aggressive moves of the land company to acquire Indian lands, and the Quakers insisted that the land could only be protected by individual ownership. In 1819 one of the missionaries reported to the committee the substance of conversations he had been having with the Indians concerning the land divisions. His letter reveals that early Seneca objections were concerned with the effect such division would have on the subsistence economy and access to resources and on the division of labor and the rights of women. We should especially note that the women emerge here, as they rarely do in Quaker reports, as directly and specifically opposed to the proposed changes.

> Many questions arose such as how will we do where
> our fields lay promiscuously or in confused division
> and all shapes & lines spliting & separating them
> & perhaps occupied by others, without a
> consideration for them. The women seemed to
> claim such parcels of land for planting corn, &
> potatoes, etc, on and the idea of a division into lots
> became very unpopular with them because they
> were sensible that clearing land was a hard task to
> perform by them & much difficulty to get their men
> to do it on account their favorite scheme cuting
> pine logs to run to market instead of the labour of
> the field for subsistence...many cut where most
> convient without control. Many think that if divided
> into lots they cannot do this & that lots that may fall
> to them will not have within its lines bottom lands
> for planting, and pine for rafting & say [the lands
> are] better owned in comnon (I.C.C.: Box 3. March
> 17, 1819).

In spite of these objections, the Quakers were encouraged
to believe they had widespread Indian support for the divisions;
but an active opposition arose in which the women figured
prominently, and the surveyor sent in by the Quakers was
ordered off Indian land. The tensions which arose over this issue
were central to the brief but violent opposition which arose in
general against the Quakers, and it is apparent that Quaker
mediation was considered less essential than was Indian judg-
ment about how best to protect their lands. In spite of repeated
calls by white men over the years for such land divisions to take
place, Seneca lands are still tribally owned.

EROSION OF POWER: THE EFFECTS OF COLONIZATION

As Seneca life changed under the influence of white society, the
power and position of Seneca women changed as well, although
they continued to control a large measure of the subsistence
production. Repeated accounts by travellers of buying corn from
Indian women would indicate that they probably derived some
small cash return through the sale of surplus produce. Women
continued to participate equally with men in overseeing the
general conduct of ritual life, and the celebration of the three
sisters of corn, beans and squash — which is the special domain

of women (Randle 1951) — further reinforced female control of these basic subsistence items. Male crops are excluded from ritual consideration.

Evidence that the important position of women was being challenged appears sporadically in the record. John Adlum, travelling among the Senecas in 1794, observes that "if the Indians go to war without the consent of the great woemen the mothers of the Sachems and Nation, The Great Spirit will not prosper them in War, but will cause them and their efforts to end in disgrace" (quoted in Kent and Deardorff 1960:465). The debate about going to war was heated and the women were adamantly opposed. Cornplanter, who was advocating the action,

> eventually got tired of the obstinacy of the Woemen and to do way (with) the superstition of the men respecting it, rose and made a speech against superstition, he called it folly and nonsense, and was surprised that men of understanding had so long submitted to this ancient custom handed down to them by their ancestors, and now was the time, for men to decide for themselves and take this power from the women (: 466).

Handsome Lake, the Seneca prophet who rose to power after 1799 and around whose teachings the current Seneca Longhouse Religion is structured, endorsed a modification in the structure of Seneca society away from matrilineal unity and toward the primacy of the nuclear family. As Wallace writes,

> It is plain that he was concerned to stabilize the nuclear family by protecting the husband-wife relationship against abrasive events. A principal abrasive, in his view, was the hierarchical relationship between a mother and her daughter. Mothers, he believed, were all too prone to urge their daughters toward sin by administering abortifacients and sterilizing medicines, by drunkenness, by practicing witchcraft, and by providing love magic....Thus, in order to stabilize the nuclear family it was necessary to loosen the tie between mother and daughter.... Although he did not directly challenge the matrilineal principle in regard to sib membership or the customs of nominating sachems, he made it plain that the nuclear family, rather than the maternal lineage,

was henceforward to be both the moral and
economic center of the behavioral universe.
(1970:284)

The final challenge to women's control came with the
replacement in 1848 of the traditional political structure of
sachems, who were appointed by the women and administered
power under their watchful eye, by a system of elected representatives. Women were disenfranchised and did not regain voting
privileges in the Seneca Nation until 1964 (Abler 1969). This
radical change in political structure, which had been advocated
and supported by white men (the Quakers prominently among
them; Abler 1967), was the culmination of the loss of female
power. As white men dealt with "chiefs" — self-appointed or
white-appointed spokesmen over whom women at best had
tenuous control — rather than with sachems — over whom
women had direct control — the action of these chiefs was
frequently independent of review by either women specifically or
the community at large. In negotiations between Indian men and
white men the intervening presence of female mediators was
unexpected and unwelcomed by the whites and inhibited the
exercise of full control by Indian men, who were observing the
independent action of white men in male-oriented American
society.

In spite of the urging of both the Quakers and Handsome
Lake for domestic reform, the pattern of brittle marriages and
serial monogamy persisted. These continued to be associated
with mobile males who engaged in a series of cash-productive
occupational specialties: hunting, lumbering and rafting, railroad
work, and the construction industries. Women continued to
form a stable sedentary base for the society, and as long as they
had primary access to resources through their persistent activity
in subsistence production, the comings and goings of men in
cash pursuits contributed to, rather than diminished, the viability
of the social unit. Women's enterprise in developing small-scale
cash-productive activities of their own, such as trading, craft
production, and, eventually, domestic service in white homes,
rendered them even more independent. But those conditions
which had so enhanced the power and position of Seneca women
in the late seventeenth and eighteenth centuries (e.g. warfare
and long-distance trade in particular), coupled with the legiti-
mate claims women had to political and economic control, were
gone. The economic options open to both men and women
became more varied, encouraging some men to become sedentary and some women more mobile. The activities of non-Quaker

missionaries intensified, but with a primary stress on conversion and behavior appropriate to Christians. Permanent settlements by whites were made in communities surrounding the reservation and on reservation land itself. This growing white population not only provided behavioral models, but also furnished local markets for the sale of Indian goods and services. Thus activities close to home increasingly became economically feasible. The structure of Seneca society came more and more to resemble that of white society, and the position of Seneca women came more and more to resemble the position of the women of the white man.

CONCLUSION

The preceding discussion, while considering the precapitalist condition of Seneca society, has focussed on the period during which white capitalism was effecting significant changes in Indian society. Through Quaker missionary intervention, the Allegany Senecas were exposed to a total program of socioeconomic development rooted in capitalist ideology, aspects of which they differentially accepted or rejected. Because the wisdom of the Quakers' program has not been questioned, and because the Quakers' behavior has not been critically examined (see, however, Berkhofer 1965), Indian responses that were contrary to Quaker proposals have been superficially interpreted as examples of counterproductive cultural conservativism. Seneca women, because they opposed modification of the traditional division of land and labor, have appeared in the literature as a particularly conservative force, and their motivation has been explanained by platitudes concerning the psychological and cultural imperatives of women in traditional societies.

On the contrary, I would contend that the apparent conservativism of Seneca women was selective and was part of a rational strategy to maintain their control of the local production which provided the subsistence base for a society dependent on a complementarity of economic sex roles. The Senecas needed more than food, and the traditional division of labor provided the means whereby they could meet the entire range of their needs. The resistance to the transferrence of agricultural production to males insured both a continued access to cash, which agricultural production in the absence of markets and transportation could not provide, and a continued female economic control upon which the influential position of women rested. That this conservativism was selective and economically rational is supported by the apparent willingness of Seneca women to accept technological innovation for both sexes. The pattern emerging from a detailed examination of the relevant documents (Rothenberg 1976a) indicates that the Senecas were attempting to keep economic options open by maximizing the flexibility of their social structure, which stemmed from its dual and complementary economic sex roles, within an environmental context of rapid and unpredictable socioeconomic change. That they did so even to the extent of jeopardizing the good will of the Quakers, whose attention was important to them, testifies to the importance that they attributed to this flexibility for the security of the community. That the Senecas are still a viable social unit with a secured land base testifies to the wisdom of their choices.

NOTES

1. Some of the material contained in this chapter appeared first in 1976 in *The Western Canadian Journal of Anthropology* (Rothenberg 1976b).

2. There has always been some problem with identifying the Senecas as strictly matrilocal. Randle remarks that "Matrilocality was the basis of the theory of the League, though habits of patrilocality and matrilocality were not well defined" (1951:170n.), although Gough reminds us that "it would be very unlikely, if not impossible, for matrilineal descent groups to develop except out of prior matrilocal residence" (1962:552). Again, the problem of structural definition may be a function of temporal variation. For the early part of the seventeenth century, the cases which Cara Richards (1957) finds documented in the *Jesuit Relations* (Thwaites 1896-1901) suggest to her a variable pattern of residence tending towards patrivirilocality, and she challenges the validity of classifying the Iroquois as matrilocal, as is done, for instance, by Murdock in the Ethnographic Atlas (1967) for the period around 1750. Both inferential and archaeological evidence suggests that matrilocality was a common residential pattern before the coming of the whites; Richards' evidence suggests that it was not during the early seventeenth century; and Morgan's sources for his evaluation of matrilocality (upon which the Murdock ratings are based) are mid-eighteenth century accounts (Morgan 1965:129-30).

Rather than reject any of these ratings, we should consider that external influences are being reflected in changing patterns of residence in accordance with Murdock's suggestions that "it is in respect to residence that changes in economy, technology, property, government, or religion first alter the structural relationships of related individuals to one another" (1949:202). The exploitation of local fur resources in the early seventeenth century ceased with the extinction of the beaver in New York in 1640 (Hunt 1940:33-34). The quest, after 1640, for new sources of fur led men into ever widening spatial explorations and produced the intensification of the condition of sedentary women and mobile men in which matrilocality is a likely residential response and of which increasing female responsibility for local affairs is a likely consequence.

3. Halliday Jackson discussed the fact that in 1799 the Indians had brought back kegs of beer from Pittsburgh when they went to sell their furs. He suggested in a footnore to this information that "a trade upon benevolent principles would be advantageously opened by friends with the Natives giving them more for their peltries than others and thus superseding the necessity of their going to a distant market. It should be a barter with useful *supplies*" (1810:122n.; emphasis in original).

4. What the Ogden Company purchased when they bought the pre-emption rights to the Seneca reservations was not land, but merely rights to purchase land which were contingent upon the Indians' willingness to sell. Unless the company could acquire the land, its investment of approximately $90,000 for these rights would have been a total loss. Thereafter, every means which the politically influential Ogdens who owned the company could use to bring pressure on the Indians to sell was used. They manipulated federal and state politics to remove the Indians to western lands, particularly to Wisconsin, Arkansas and Kansas; they bribed individual Indians and advisers of Indians; and they offered a series of alternative suggestions by which they could acquire the more valuable reservation lands in the northern part of New York State, particularly those around Buffalo and Rochester, and remove all the Senecas to the comparatively worthless land of the Allegany reservation. It was not until 1842 that the company acquired the valuable lands it sought, and this process of acquisition is amply documented in various accounts (e.g., Society of Friends 1840).

REFERENCES

Abler, Thomas S. 1967. "Seneca National Factionalism: The First Twenty Years." In E. Tooker, *Iroquois Culture, History and Prehistory, Proceedings of the 1965 Conference on Iroquois Research.* Albany: New York State Museum.

_____. 1969. *Factional Dispute and Party Conflict in the Political System of the Seneca Nation (1845-1895): An Ethnohistorical Analysis.* Toronto: National Library of Canada (microfilm).

Adams, W., ed. 1893 *Historical Gazeteer and Biographical Memorial of Cattaraugus County, New York.* Syracuse: Lyman, Horton & Co. Ltd.

Allinson, William. 1809. "Journal of William Allinson of Burlington" (ms.). Haverford, Pa.: Haverford College.

American State Papers. 1832. Class 1, Indian Affairs, Vol. 1. Washington, D.C.: National Archives.

Berkhofer, Robert F. 1965. *Salvation and the Savage: An Analysis of Protestant Missions and American Indian Response 1778-1862.* Lexington: University of Kentucky Press.

Brown, Judith. 1970. "Economic Organization and the Position of Women among the Iroquois." *Ethnohistory* 17, 3-4:151-67.

Carr, Lucien. 1883. "On the Social and Political Position of Women among the Huron-Iroquois Tribes." *Harvard University Peabody Museum of Archaeology and Ethnology Report,* no. 16, pp. 207-32.

Ember, Carol. 1974. "An Evaluation of Alternative Theories of Matrilocal versus Patrilocal Residence." *Behavior Science Research* 9,2.

_____ and Melvin Ember. 1971. "The Conditions Favoring Matrilocal vs. Patrilocal Residence." *American Anthropolgist* 73:3:571-594.

Everett, Edward A., Chairman. 1922. *Report of the New York State Indian Commission to Investigate the Status of the American Indian Residing in the State of New York.* Albany: New York State Legislature, March 17, 1922. Privately printed in 1972.

Freilich, Morris. 1958. "Cultural Persistence among the Modern Iroquois." *Anthropos* 53:473-83.

Gough, Kathleen. 1962. "Variations in Residence." In D.M. Schneider and K. Gough, eds., *Matrilineal Kinship.* Berkeley and Los Angeles: University of California Press.

Harder, John F. 1963. "The Indian Policy of Henry Knox 1785-1794." M.A. thesis, University of Wisconsin-Milwaukee.

Heckewelder, John. 1817. *History, Manners, and Customs of the Indian Nations.* Philadelphia: Historical Society of Pennsylvania.

Hedrick, Ulysses P. 1933. *A History of Agriculture in the State of New York.* New York: State Agricultural Society.

Hertzberg, Hazel. 1971. *The Search for an American Indian Identity: Modern Pan-Indian Movements.* Syracuse: Syracuse University Press.

Hunt, George. 1940. *The Wars of the Iroquois: A Study of Intertribal Trade Relations.* Madison: University of Wisconsin Press.

Indian Committee Collection (I.C.C.). Philadelphia Yearly Meeting Archives. Philadelphia, Pa.: Friends' Book Store.

Jackson, Halliday. 1806-1818. "Journals" (mss.) West Chester, Pa. : Chester County Historical Society.

_____. 1830. *Civilization of the Indian Natives*. Philadelphia: Marcus T.C. Gould.

Jacobs, Wilbur. 1950. *Wilderness Politics and Indian Gifts: The Northern Colonial Frontier 1748-1763*. Lincoln: University of Nebraska Press.

Kent, Donald H., and Merle H. Deardorff. 1960. "John Adlum on the Allegheny: Memoirs for the Year 1794." *Pennsylvania Magazine of History and Biography* 84, 3-4.

Kussart, Serepta. 1938. *The Allegheny River*. Pittsburgh, Pa.: Burgum Printing Co.

"McAllister Collection" (mss.). Philadelphia: Historical Society of Pennsylvania.

Morgan, Lewis H. 1851. *League of the Ho-De-No-Sau-Nee, or, Iroquois*. New York: Dodd, Mead & Co.

_____ . 1965. (orig. 1881). *Houses and House-Life of the American Aborigines*. Chicago: University of Chicago Press.

Murdock, George P. 1949. *Social Structure*. New York: Macmillan Co.

_____. 1967. *Ethnographic Atlas*. Pittsburgh: University of Pittsburgh Press.

Noon, James A. 1949. "Law and Government of the Grand River Iroquois." The Viking Fund, Inc. No. 12.

Norton, Major John. 1970. *The Journal of Major John Norton (1809-1816)*, Carl F. Klinck and James J. Tolman, eds. The Publications of the Champlain Society, vol. 46. Toronto: Champlain Society.

Parker, Arthur C. 1912. "Iroquois Uses of Maize and Other Food Plants." *New York State Museum Bulletin*, no. 144. Albany: University of the State of New York.

Quain, Buell. 1937. "The Iroquois." In M. Mead, ed., *Cooperation and Competition among Primitive People*. New York: McGraw-Hill.

Randle, Martha. 1951. "Iroquois Women Then and Now." In W. Fenton, ed., Symposium on Local Diversity in Iroquois Culture. Washington: Bureau of American Ethnology, Bulletin No. 149.

Richards, Cara. 1957. "Matriarchy or Mistake: The Role of Iroquois Women through Tiime." In V. Ray, ed., *Cultural Stability and Culture Change*. Proceedings of the Annual Meeting of the American Ethnological Society, Seattle, Washington.

_____. 1967. "Huron and Iroquois Residence Patterns 1600-1650." In E. Tooker, ed., *Iroquois Culture, History and Prehistory, Proceedings of the 1965 Conference on Iroquois Research*. Albany: New York State Museum.

Rothenberg, Diane B. 1976a. *Friends Like These: An Ethnohistorical Analysis of the Interaction Between Allegany Senecas and Quakers, 1798-1823*. Ann Arbor, Mich.: University Microfilms.

_____. 1976b. "Erosion of Power: An Economic Basis for the Selective Conservatism of Seneca Women in the Nineteenth Century." *Western Canadian Journal of Anthropology* 6,3.

Seaver, James E. 1961. (orig. 1824) *A Narrative of the Life of Mrs. Mary Jemison, The White Woman of the Genesee.* New York: Corinth Books.

Shimony, Annemarie. 1961. "Conservatism among the Iroquois at the Six Nations Reserve." *Yale University Publications in Anthropplogy,* no.65.

Skinner, Dorothy P. 1929. "Seneca Notes Collected on the Allegheny Reservation, New York, 1928, and Cornplanter Reservation, Pennsylvania, 1929" (ms.). James Prendergast Library, Jamestown, N.Y.

Snyderman, George S. 1961. "Concepts of Land Ownership among the Iroquois and Their Neighbors." In W. Fenton, ed., Symposium on Local Diversity in Iroquois Culture. Washington: Bureau of American Ethnology, Bulletin No. 149.

Society of Friends. 1840. *Statement of Facts for the Information of Our Own Members, in Relation to the Circumstances of the Seneca Indians in the State of New York.* Philadelphia.

Stites, Sara H. 1905. *Economics of the Iroquois.* Bryn Mawr College Mongraph Series, Vol. 1, No. 3. Lancaster, Pa.: New Era Printing Co.

Sydney, James V. 1963. *A People Among People: Quaker Benevolence in Eighteenth Century America.* Cambridge, Mass.: Harvard University Press.

Thwaites, Reuben G., ed. 1896-1901. *The Jesuit Relations and Allied Documents.* Cleveland, Ohio: Burrows.

Tuck, James A. 1971. "The Iroquois Confederacy." *Scientific American* 224, 3:32-42.

Wallace, Anthony F.C. 1957. "Political Organization and Land Tenure among the Northeastern Indians 1600-1830." *Southwestern Journal of Anthropology* 13:301-21.

_____. 1970. *The Death and Rebirth of the Seneca: The History and Culture of the Great Iroquois Nation, Their Destruction and Demoralization, and Their Cultural Revival at the Hands of the Indian Visionary, Handsome Lake.* New York: Alfred A. Knopf.

Washburn, Wilcomb E. 1971. *Red Man's Land —White Man's Law: A Study of the Past and Present Status of the American Indian.* New York: Charles Scribner's Sons.

Whipple, J.S., Chairman. 1889. *Report of the Special Committee to Investigate the Indian Problem of the State of New York Appointed by the Assembly of 1888.* Albany: Troy Press Co.

White, Marian. 1961. "Iroquois Culture History in the Niagara Frontier Area." Museum of Anthropology, Anthropological Paper no. 24. Ann Arbor: University of Michigan.

Wrenshall, John. 1816. "The John Wrenshall Journal" (ms.). Pittsburgh: Historical Society of Western Pennsylvania.

SOCIAL ART/SOCIAL ACTION

On Mother's Day in 1984, 154 older women dressed in white assembled around white-covered tables in the Children's Cove on the beach in La Jolla, California. Against the backdrop of the Pacific Ocean, the blue sky, and swooping seagulls, they talked about the problems and pleasures of aging. Three years later on Mother's Day 1987, 430 older women dressed in black sat at tables which formed color squares against a black carpeted background. Under the faceted windows covering the prestigious courtyard of the central commercial building of downtown Minneapolis, the women formed a "living quilt" and talked again about the pleasures and problems of aging. Although the visual images were dramatically different, the connections between the two performances are obvious. Both the California *Whisper, The Waves, The Wind* and the Minnesota *Crystal Quilt* were conceived and executed by the artist Suzanne Lacy and are thematically related to her ongoing concern with creating artworks that address major social issues and give voice to the disadvantaged, ignored women of contemporary American society. Both were elaborate performances requiring the assistance of many people and the expenditure of much money during extensive preparation periods. And both had the rather unusual attention of a resident anthropologist engaged in the classical anthropological fieldwork practice of participant observation.

In 1983 I was glad to respond to Lacy's invitation to serve on an advisory board for the Whisper Project, but then requested that I be permitted to extend my participation toward a scholarly study of the structure of the organization being formed to facilitate the performance. I was interested in many issues, but especially in the preparation process and in the development of an organization of volunteers oriented toward expediting a specific and unfamiliar goal. My primary focus, then, was on issues of social organization and process, but ancillary interests were relevant and included a desire to examine feminist contentions about female collaborative art making as distinct from the patriarchal model of the autonomous artist. I also wished to explore the manifest and latent symbolic content and the cultural metaphors embedded in both the performance and in the

Original publication in T.D.R. *(The Drama Review)*, Volume 32, no. 1, Spring 1988.

preparation as performance, and to examine how the symbols were manipulated and expressed toward goal realization.

Because I was resident in San Diego County during the months of preparation for the La Jolla performance, I was able to observe all aspects of the process, assist in the performance, and then for six subsequent months, carry on a series of extended interviews with about twenty-five participants and observers of the La Jolla event. The opportunity to study the Minneapolis project was welcome for the purpose of comparing and contrasting the events, but the fieldwork was conducted during two short visits in early February and in mid-May 1987, so I had to rely more heavily on interviews than on observation. I have come to regard the Whisper Project, in both of its manifestations, as "demonstration projects" for feminist experiments in manipulating the social world, as well as provocative case studies for issues relating to "community" art.

Lacy believes in the possibility of changing the world through art making — not in the slow, incremental influence on the consciousness of the cognoscenti, but in the direct appeal to a mass audience. For Lacy there is a continual push in the direction of making works public and accessible because of the urgency of the message contained. The gesture is populist, as is much of the performance art emanating from a feminist orientation; Lacy has a vision of an expanded audience that includes those not familiar with contemporary art and not accustomed to acccepting political stimuli to action through art. Although aesthetic issues are paramount for her and are available for discussion within the art world, her overt message is not about art — it is about society. Her proposed audience is not the hermetic art world, though they are certainly invited — it is society. The performance is neither performed by nor is it about the artist, though her personal mythology creates the image and the vision which informs it. Following a tradition already well established by decades of art moves (e.g., "happenings") Lacy avoids the spaces of art galleries and museums and the neighborhoods of art enclaves, mounting her pieces in well-used public spaces. She publicizes her performances through whatever popular medium she can attract; the use and manipulation of the media is one aspect of the overall "demonstration project" nature of the work.

Lacy's populism extends to her coworkers; she includes as significant participants people for whom artworks have little interest and makes available a menu of goals and rewards from which they can choose the reason for their ongoing involvement in her project. Her success in attracting and keeping participants over long periods of time testifies to the relevance of her concerns in the social sphere, to her skills at social organization, and to her ability to make pieces which are accessible. She addresses the issue of the alienation of the avant-garde by advocating social change in a form that broadens the audience for art statements.

Unlike performances which have theatrical or art-historical references, Lacy's preferred referential system dates to pageantry, and particularly to those pageants of the nineteenth and early twentiethth centuries created by women and addressed to vital social concerns such as women's suffrage and war protest. The tradition is a content-oriented form in which the statement is conveyed through a static image — the *tableau vivant.* The image which carries the message is culturally loaded and multivocal; it certainly has no finite reading, but contains something for everyone. It is nondiscursive, nondevelopmental, nondramatic in form; there is no building to a climax.

Both Whisper Project performances progressed from art into life as the stunning image was broken by the audience, which was invited to intrude, and as the performers were reabsorbed from their liminal condition of isolation and elevation into real life, embodied by the audience. In La Jolla, the ceremonious processional of elderly women onto the beach and their recessional to the waiting buses structured a bounded performance for the observing audience. For the audience members who had chosen a more active engagement and had joined the women on the beach to interact with them and with each other in conversation, the performance ended whenever they chose to conclude their intention.

In Minneapolis, the elderly women were assembled on four sides of the performance space and released in groups, filling one or two tables at a time. The careful orchestration produced the impression that women were casually assembling, and from the audience it was difficult to say precisely when the performance began. The conclusion would seem to have been the moment before the audience joined the women in the performance space to congratulate and celebrate them, but the assembling and mingling was symbolically and structurally intrinsic to the performance itself. It should be noted, however, that the timing and sequencing of both performances were highly orchestrated and directed by Lacy from a central viewing area. All production people were trained to respond to pre-set musical clues in the taped original compositions by Susan Stone. Further, an elaborate intercom system had been set up so that Lacy could communicate with the production staff, and they with selected others, in order to precisely control the sequence of events. This same system could be used for any emergencies that might arise (but fortunately did not), and medical assistants were prepared to respond appropriately and discreetly so as not to disrupt the performance. Both performances, which appeared to flow so effortlessly and spontaneously, were highly controlled and structured events.

The several hours of each performance contained a richness of data and multivocal symbols. There were references to issues of women/nature/culture in, for instance, the choice of white (in La Jolla) and black (in Minneapolis), and in the choice of natural environment (La Jolla) as against social/architectural space (Minneapolis). References to ritual were suggested by the processional and recessional in La Jolla, the orchestrated arm movements in Minneapolis, and by the ceremoniousness of movement in both cases; also, the framing of the women as interacting isolates, separated from their world of daily occurrence, implied a certain liminality and communitas (to use Victor Turner's useful concepts [see Turner 1982]). Particularly when the audience replaced the women on the beach in La Jolla, there was a hint at issues of generation sequencing and replacement. Lacy's use of the public media and the obvious presence of cameras and media people at both performances werenot merely instrumenal but also symbolically reflexive, pointing as they did to the power of the media in shaping our perception of the world.

The performances themselves were the culminating events for two long periods of preparation, and it is to the organization of this preparation that I would like to direct some attention. The scale of the two performances determined the extent of the organization and of the finances that were required to effect them. But the scale was an arbitrary factor and escalated during the process of preparation, at least in La Jolla. This set up a tension between expectation and the possibility of realization that highly informed the preparation period. An invitation for a two-week residency was extended to Lacy by the Center for Music Experiment on the campus of the University of California-San Diego in La Jolla. Lacy finalized the negotiations in April 1983. The mandate was to construct a performance, out of a workshop preparation, that would outreach to the "community" of people who did not often attend events sponsored by the Center. The budget of $4,000 was provided through a National Endowment for the Arts grant. During the period of negotiations, Lacy conceived the image of the figures on the beach and recognized that she needed more time and more money to realize the performance. The Center for Music Experiment was willing to extend the time and to endorse the project, but not to provide further funding. The notion of community outreach was intrinsic to its interests and appealing to Lacy's own sense of populist performance. She expected to turn to the anticipated La Jolla/San Diego community for participation, on all levels of endorsement — personal, financial, and institutional — and she certainly secured some of each. But San Diego was a difficult place to secure funding, to acquire stable and committed volunteer assistance over an extended period of time, and to attract performers for a number of reasons: the geographic dispersement of population throughout San Diego County; the social, geographic, and economic isolation of population enclaves (e.g., the relative wealth of La Jolla in contrast with the urban economies of the city of San Diego); the relative lack of complex social networks with which a population of newcomers connects; the absence of social symbols of unity through established institutions and recognized social leaders identified with place; and the lack of connection and commitment of local business in supporting public events and symbols. It was also an inopportune place to make a convincing case that the performance would generate a lasting place-specific symbol for future sociopolitical action.

The period from initiation to final performance in La Jolla was just a month over one year. An organization was sufficiently established and functioning to effect an intermediate performance, the *Pot Luck*, in October of 1983. The purposes of this event were multiple: it satisfied the terms of the original grant requiring a community event within that year; it gave publicity to the overall project and an opportunity to initiate media attention; it called attention to the recruitment needs for the future performance; it allowed women to interact with each other in a joyous and commemorative way; and it provided an occasion for the production staff to hone skills that would be required later. Expenses were minimal: the women brought the food they shared, the space was donated, and the preparation was not elaborate. For those older women who comprised the Steering Committee, it provided an incentive to actively recruit from their extensive networks for the culminating performance. The eighteen women on the committee were, in one way or another, all community activists. They represented a wide range of ethnic and racial backgrounds and so had access to diverse segments of the San Diego population. Of this group, perhaps half continued active participation throughout the duration of the project, and somewhat fewer than half were featured in the various visual and auditory presentations of the work. In follow-up discussions, all agreed that they had benefited from participation and that the project, although more demanding on their time and attention than they had anticipated, had been worthwhile — but none were prepared to develop an organization or other projects to continue the message or activities past the *Whisper, the Waves, the Wind* performance.

Organizational issues, including fund-raising and re-cruitment of both personnel and performers, went on until the day of the performance in May 1984. The projected budget climbed from the original $4,000 grant to several thousand over $100,000 in cash, with an additional $60,000 required to produce a film that was not part of the initial plan. The film was finally finished, in part because contributions were made in Minneapolis toward its completion. The budget of $100,000 was a dream and less than half of that amount was raised, although in-kind contributions made a difference. Of the approximately $40,000 spent in cash, a substantial amount was contributed by Lacy from her own resources, and the hope that some salaries could be paid was abandoned. Donors were encouraged to honor a woman by sponsoring, for $250, a chair in her name; about fifty- five such donations were made. There were some corporate donations, but it was not anticipated that the total from this source would amount to more than about $10,000, and the final amount was considerably less. The desire to effect the most fully realized performance without aesthetic compromise entailed the ongoing escalation of costs as production problems were perceived and addressed.

Recruitment of performers was similarly unpredictable. An earnest effort to recruit was carried on continually, but my notes of mid-April 1984 reveal the frustration that members of the steering committee were experiencing in their efforts to interest people in participating. They suggested that "people who think they are secure don't want to stir the waters," and "older people don't want to be involved with older people." Lacy, in response to these remarks, suggested that "activists must find the button to push." In spite of the recruitment effort, by the week before the performance there was little assurance that more than about sixty women had committed themselves to appear. The hope that no performer would have been without some prepara-tion and rehearsal necessarily gave way to the reality that women who had never been seen before would show up on the day of the performance. That is what happened. Women appeared appar-ently from nowhere, brought by others and attracted by the publicity. The prearranged congregating area was in the dining toom of a retirement community, and one of the residents, seeing the women in white assembled, rushed upstairs to change her clothes and become one of the group. A core of women, mostly those on the steering committee, knew the sequence of events, and they were able to give some direction to the others, but it was the high degree of preparation and coordination of the production staff that made possible the smooth flow of the largely unrehearsed performers.

The Minneapolis experience was sharply contrastive, both because of the nature of the place and because Lacy's prior experience suggested strategies for avoiding problems. She was invited by the Minneapolis College of Art and Design for a six-month residency to begin in September '84, and accepted the invitation with the intention of developing a series of three or four thematically related pieces relevant to Minnesota and leading to the large, culminating performance nearly three years later in 1987. The scale was anticipated from the beginning, and Lacy knew that an in-place, germinal organization was a prerequisite for beginning work.

During the first of the three years, Lacy spoke to many people both formally and informally to generate interest, initiating the process of developing an organization to effect the project. This was accomplished by August of 1985. The original plan of multiple performances around the state with a projected budget of $200,000 was recognized as unrealistic, and strategy was changed to directly focus on The *Crystal Quilt* preparations and to concurrently encourage several different kinds of activities. For example, in the summer of 1986 a videotaping project was accomplished at the state fair. It was feared that women would be reluctant to appear in front of the camera and address themselves to prepared questions but, in fact, long lines of waiting women formed. Lacy also initiated the *Season's Project,* a collaborative photographic project located in Duluth and involving photographers and a sound composer with the goal of developing a series of photographs of Minnesota women against the changing background of the seasonal Minnesota environment. As of September 1987, two seasons had already been completed and the work was continuing.

Lacy's strategy was to seek prior community support. The challenge was to demonstrate that both the project and the artist were place specific — that the project would address and enhance life in Minnesota. The support and interest of several leading institutions (including the Minneapolis College of Art and Design, the Minnesota Council on Aging, and The Humphrey Institute of the University of Minnesota, among others) as well as of recognized community leaders, together with Lacy's three-year residency in Minneapolis, stimulated those waves of additional support that were essential. Relevant, too, is the Minnesotan expectation that local business be involved in community affairs.

One socially prominent fund-raiser told me that corporate newcomers are frequently startled to learn that they will be expected to actively engage, that the question they are asked is "how much" not "whether."

The scaled-back budget for the three-year Minnesota project was finally about $170,000 in cash and roughly another $200,000 in in-kind contributions. A large in-kind contribution, for instance, was the space donated by B.C.E.D. Properties, Inc., in the prestigious I.D.S. Building, to be used for project offices, as well as access to the Crystal Court for the performance and its preparation. The enhancement of administrative and organizational capability, not to mention the psychological lift that an official space provided, was incalculable and would have been financially impossible without the donation. Of the $170,000 raised, about ten percent came from various state government grants, about eighteen percent from individual contributions ranging from $15,000 to $1, and about 72 percent from corporations and foundations. The largest single corporate contribution was made by the medical supply company, Medtronic Foundation, for $35,000, but some corporate contributions were as low as $500.

The public performance was effected by an organization largely composed of volunteer women, and it is estimated that about 1,500 women in all participated. Of that number, more than half were older women. Several full-time positions in administration and management were paid — these responsibilities required a continuity of time and attention that would have been unrealistic to expect from volunteers. Several volunteer positions were converted to minimally paid positions as tasks developed, but also, it seemed, as personal needs were perceived and addressed. All paid personnel had begun as volunteers and thus had complex interests and investments in the success of the project. In total there were fifteen administrative positions, of which seven were paid through stipends. Three of these seven employees were older women. During the several weeks preceding the performance in May, forty-seven short-term key positions existed, twenty-seven of which were paid and included four older women.

Most of the participants were volunteers and, as with voluntarism in general, a sensitivity toward meeting hidden agendas and furnishing rewards was essential. The negotiation of personal needs, of "stroking," of attention paid, created a complicated dynamic in an organization created to carry out an artist's personal vision. Participants had to personalize the goal, or some part of it, as their own, had to be allowed some degree of autonomy and self-expression if they desired it, and had to be made to feel essential to the realization of a project that was worth realizing. They had to be given some control, but for that to happen, Lacy had to relinquish some control. She had to do this because the scale she had established necessitated relying on others. At the same time, she worried, not without cause, that she was losing control over the execution of a vision that was ultimately hers and for which she would be held accountable. The give and take in these situations provided an opportunity for a kind of collusion of the group against Lacy as authority figure — which probably bound the participants more closely together.

At the same time, the participants were bound to Lacy by feelings of affection and sympathy. They recognized the effort she was making, the strain she was under, the willingness on her part to negotiate what moments before seemed nonnegotiable. The expectation and the willingness to become emotionally demonstrative and nurturing probably underlie much of the success of women's attempts at collaborative art.

The nature of the task called not only for the learning of new skills by many of the women but for an intensification and redefinition of old ones. Women with previously proven skills, particularly in management and fund-raising, were sought out, but others found that their domestic skills could be redirected toward specific employment-related activities, e.g., fund-raising, publicity and public relations, various levels of management, and general social networking.

Skills alone, however, could not realize the project. What was needed was money, and the acquisition and manipulation of money took on the quality of a cultural metaphor through the entire preparation period, particularly of the La Jolla project. Some part of the "demonstration project" nature of the preparation period seemed to be addressed to exploring issues of women, money, and power, and of the woman artist and society. Being able to raise money indicated Lacy's (and by extension, women's) power in the world; her inability to raise what she needed demonstrated the establishment's lack of support for women artists (represented by, but not limited to, Lacy), for women in general, and particularly for the powerless group of elderly women who were the subject of the piece.

Many of the tensions that arose during the preparation period in La Jolla were specifically centered around Lacy's expectation that all would participate in fund-raising — particularly the fifteen or so women who constituted the Support Committee — and the rejection of that idea by most of the women. It was fascinating to watch women volunteering labor, space, time; willing to prepare brunches, teas, receptions; willing to make things, clean things, cook things; but absolutely unwilling or unable either to contribute money they could define as their own, or to ask the same of others. The reasons for this unwillingness are probably multiple and complex. The possibility exists that the surface opulence of California life disguises limited financial resources, that women understood that entering into a relationship with others to solicit money would require future reciprocity, and that the ability to contribute suggested a differential class placement and inequality that were in sharp contrast to the egalitarian relationships being established through co-participation. Probably, for some, the public distribution of money had always been in male hands. Two or three women finally declared themselves open to experimenting with fund-raising, and were given training in appropriate solicitation techniques.

The Minnesota project reflected an explicit message of "empowerment," which permeated the preparation and the performance. A novel program in the development of leadership skills was conducted through the Reflective Leadership Program of the Humphrey Institute of the University of Minnesota and was organized as the Older Women's Leadership Program. Thirty-five older women were targeted and enrolled. Seventeen of these were from beyond the urban area and the group as a whole represented a wide range of ethnic backgrounds. The average age was seventy-four and the age range was from sixty to eighty-eight. Although the program did not specifically address the needs of the Whisper Project, all thirty-five subsequently entered the project as participants and provided their networks of social contacts throughout the state. Thirty of these women appeared as performers in *The Crystal Quilt.*

Minnesota was a gratifying environment in which to work. Social networks tended to be complex and of long standing. People identified with the place and particularly with the social climate oriented toward accepting personal responsibility for group efforts — a trait proudly asserted as intrinsic to the Minnesota (i.e., Scandinavian) heritage. There was an active and assertive expectation that the effort involved in the development of the performance would be only a first step toward future action addressing the issues of aging that would be carried on by local people after Lacy's work had ended. An organization was founded by ten of the women who, several days later, would be in the performance. All of them had met through the Whisper Project and five had been in the Older Women's Leadership Program.

Currently, this group has decided to address itself to

Diane Rothenberg

challenging stereotypes of older women and plans to offer a series around the state to train older women in community-oriented leadership skills. They are considering undertaking several research projects, one of which would involve touring rural areas to document the lives of women through in-depth interviewing. On 29 August 1987 in Minneapolis they took part in a panel at a major conference, "Take Back the Night," addressing issues of violence against women, and they decided to participate through lectures and demonstrations in a later area conference sponsored by the Minnesota Council on Aging.

The above analysis would seem to suggest that the Minnesota performance was the more successful of the two, and by the criteria of social action it probably was. In fact, I do not believe the factors that I have discussed informed the aesthetic experience in either case. The culminating performances were complex, aesthetically satisfying experiences in both cases. They addressed a significant social issue, and they did so in a way that engaged a local population in a place-specific manner. In La Jolla the elemental aspects of sea, sun, beach, birds, and women in white came closer to approaching a condition of transformation and liminality. In Minneapolis, the imagery was rooted in the social aspects of women's lives and particularly of Minnesotan women's lives. They wore the black of elderly experience, they composed a living quilt and stitched it with the orchestrated movements of their arms. They were protected from the world of nature by the world of culture and social structure inherent in the architecture of a commercial center. Both images of women are true and complimentary; in both places the women revealed thoughts and experiences of elderly women which are seldom revealed; and both performances created a context in which the voices of these women could be raised from a whisper to a shout.

REFERENCE

Turner, Victor. 1982. *From Ritual to Theater and Back.* New York: PAJ Publications.

CORN SOUP & FRY BREAD

For several years before and for two inclusive years from 1972 to 1974, we lived on the Allegany Seneca Reservation in Salamanca, New York. Food was among the first things we exchanged, poetry only later and never really fully. From our end the items served were dishes such as sukiyaki or pumpernickel rye; from theirs the common foods of rural America and two specially prepared dishes that indicated that a uniquely Native American festivity was underway. One of those dishes was "corn soup" (more specifically "hulled corn soup" [hominy], because there are other ways of using corn in soups), and the other one was "fry bread." During the years that we lived in Salamanca, we encountered both of these dishes many times and in variant versions. Different people whom we knew approached their preparation in individualized ways, congruent always with their own tastes, their interest in food preparation, and their concern (or lack of it) with "authenticity." When we reproduce those dishes now for special occasions of our own, these same considerations inform our sense of how to go about it. As a reflection on the issue of "authenticity" in the preparation of traditional foods — as well as the contribution of a couple of good recipes to round out the present volume — I offer up the following.

"AUTHENTIC" HULLED CORN SOUP à la Archie Johnson, who knows how to do many things the "old way."

1 quart dry corn
1 pint clean hardwood ashes
Water to cover

Place in cast iron kettle and bring to a boil. Boil until the hulls slip off the kernels (about 20 minutes). Place in corn basket, and rinse in cold water until clean. Reboil corn in water until suds form, and rinse again in basket. Repeat once more.

3/4 lb. salt pork cut up
1/4 lb. dried red kidney beans (pre-soaked)
Prepared corn (hominy) from first step

Boil all together in kettle for 3 or 4 hours. Makes about 4 quarts of soup.

"CONVENIENT" HULLED CORN SOUP à la Richard Johnny John, who loves it but, for all kinds of reasons, takes short cuts.

3 large cans of hominy (undrained)
1 can of red beans (undrained)
1 lb. pork (or maybe more if using spareribs)

Water enough to create a thick soup. Cook everything together until the pork is done.

"ROTHENBERG" HULLED CORN SOUP, being a variation of Dick Johnny John's recipe, but accommodating to non-Seneca expectations.

2 lbs. of pork with bones
1 carrot
Couple of handfulls of celery and celery tops
1 onion
Parsley
Salt and pepper to taste
Water to cover

Cook until pork is separating from bones. Drain through a strainer, and save the pieces of meat.

3 large cans of hominy (undrained)
1 can of red beans (undrained)

Combine broth, pork, and canned ingredients, and cook together for a few minutes. Season to taste.

FRY BREAD is known among the Senecas as "Ghost Bread," because it is always included in the feast that follows the ten days of mourning after a death. A look at the ingredients suggests immediately that even the "authentic" version depends entirely on store-bought ingredients; yet fry bread, with minor variations in shape and ingredients, is emblematically "Indian" all through North America.

2 cups white flour
3 tsp. baking powder
2 tblsp. sugar

Pinch salt
1 cup water

Knead together, and let stand for 15 minutes. Break off golf ball sized pieces, and roll each out, using flour to prevent sticking. Stab with a fork twice through the center of each. Fry in deep fat until brown on both sides. Eat hot.

FRY BREAD à la Thelma Shane, one of the best cooks around.

Same as above but add along with other ingredients:

2 tblsp. oil
1/2 small can crushed pineapple.

Proceed as above. Roll out 1/2 inch thick, and fry until brown. (Thelma usually serves these with margarine and pre-serves, accompanied regularly by coffee.)

"FAST FRY BREAD," which is what you usually get at our feasts. This recipe was revealed to us at an Indian Foods Dinner — a tourist-oriented feast offered, as a fund-raiser, around Thanksgiving, i.e. harvest time. One or another Seneca organization is allowed to prepare the dinner each year, at which time they serve hundreds of diners, both white and Indian, who have reserved well in advance, eager for the opportunity to taste the variety and abundance of "authentic" Seneca food. The Senecas with whom we ate would snicker a little when fry bread was presented in the following way:

Open a tube of store-bought prepared biscuits (not the sourdough type, but it hardly matters). Separate the biscuits, and flatten each, using a little flour to prevent sticking. Pierce with the tines of a fork, and fry in deep fat. They rise and brown very quickly, so keep watching. Drain and serve.

With a genuine taste for the inauthentic (as much as for its counterpart), we have made this recipe our own.

Printed February 1992 by Cushing-Malloy
Inc., Ann Arbor. Design & typesetting by
Pierre Joris on a Macintosh IIsi using
Page Maker 4, at Ta'wil Books &
Documents, Encinitas.

DIANE ROTHENBERG is the author of *Friends Like These: An Ethnohistorical Analysis of the Interaction Between Allegany Senecas and Quakers 1798-1823* (1976) and co-editor of *Symposium of the Whole: A Range of Discourse Toward an Ethnopoetics* (1983). Early into an ethnohistorical approach to anthropology, she has been a critic of a narrow cultural model while exploring the concept of the human being as rational actor. Her writings have investigated issues of gender and aging, ritual and art, communities and community formation, and she has been an active player in the discourse around an emerging ethnopoetics. She received a doctorate in anthropology from the Graduate Center of the City University (New York) and has taught anthropology and related subjects at the University of Wisconsin - Milwaukee, SUNY - Albany, SUNY - Binghamton, the University of Southern California, and the University of California at San Diego. For two years (1972-1974) she lived at the Allegany Seneca Reservation in Salamanca, New York.